An Introduction to
Prayer

An Introduction to
Prayer

Bishop Robert Barron

W✦RD *on* FIRE.

Published by Word on Fire,
Elk Grove Village, IL 60007

© 2024 by Word on Fire Catholic Ministries
Printed in the United States of America
All rights reserved

Cover design, typesetting, and interior art direction by Michael Stevens,
Clark Kenyon, and Rozann Lee

ISBN: 978-1-68578-146-0

Library of Congress Control Number: 2024934033

Contents

Part IV: Contemplative Prayer

Part V: Liturgical Prayer

Part VI: Devotional Prayer

Part VII: Scriptural Prayer

Preface

POPE FRANCIS HAS DESIGNATED 2025 as a Year of Jubilee, and in preparation for that celebration, he has, in turn, designated 2024 as a Year of Prayer. It is in response to the pope's call for renewed catechesis on prayer that Word on Fire presents this small collection of texts from my writings and talks on the subject.

Though I certainly prayed as a child and attended Mass every Sunday with my parents, I did not become fascinated with prayer until, as a teenager, I came across the works of Thomas Merton, especially *The Seven Storey Mountain*, *Seeds of Contemplation*, and *The Sign of Jonas*. These marvelous books opened my mind and heart to the mystical tradition stretching from the biblical authors, through the Fathers of the Church, up to figures such as Bernard, Teresa of Avila, Meister Eckhart, and especially John of the Cross. And Merton's own witness made that tradition come alive for a young man eager to find his way to speak to God. Another very important step on my itinerary of prayer was my first visit to St. Meinrad Archabbey just weeks before my ordination to the priesthood. Though I had heard recordings of monastic chant before, I had never actually experienced the sound and texture of that ancient form of song. I will never forget the moment when I entered the abbey church, a little late for Morning Prayer, and heard those seventy voices crying out harmoniously and longingly for God.

Perhaps my greatest teachers in the way of prayer have been the people whom I have served in the course of my pastoral ministry. How often as a priest I have heard the plaintive cry "Father, pray for me!" or "Father, pray for my mom, who has just gone into the hospital" or "Father, pray for my kids; they're feeling kind of lost." Those urgent requests taught me a lesson that John Paul II knew very well: at the end of the day, all prayer is a form of petition. They also compelled me to see that authentic prayer *always* connects us to others in love.

My hope for this little book is very simple: that it might lead you on the road to prayer; that it might teach you something about prayer; and that, most importantly, it might prompt you actually to pray. And take great comfort, as I do, from this saying of St. Josemaría Escrivá: "You say you don't know how to pray? Put yourself in the presence of God, and once you have said, 'Lord, I don't know how to pray!' rest assured that you have begun to do so."

Part I

What Is Prayer?

Raising the Mind and Heart to God

PEOPLE PRAY ALL THE TIME. Studies show that even those who describe themselves as nonbelievers pray. What precisely is this activity in which so many of us willingly engage? Prayer has taken on myriad forms over the centuries. Speaking, processing, singing, remaining silent, emptying the mind of all imagery and conceptuality, reading sacred texts, dancing, and petitioning from the bottom of one's heart have all been construed as modalities of prayer. But is there a common denominator, some fundamental characteristic? St. John of Damascus, a monk and theologian from the eighth century, said, "Prayer is the raising of one's mind and heart to God," and St. Thérèse of Lisieux said that prayer is "a surge of the heart, it is a simple look towards Heaven, it is a cry of recognition and of love, embracing both trial and joy." Prayer is born of that awareness, felt more than thought, that the transcendent realm impinges on our lowly world and hence can be contacted. A basic Christian conviction is that this reaching for God meets an even more passionate divine reaching for us. Perhaps we would put it best by saying that the mystical coming together of these two longings—our longing for God and God's longing for us—is prayer.

I don't know any other place on earth that evokes the power of prayer more than the magnificent Sainte-Chapelle in Paris. Built by King Louis IX (St. Louis) in the thirteenth century as a grand repository for the relic of Jesus' crown of thorns, the Sainte-Chapelle is a jewel box of stained glass and Gothic tracery. When you enter the building, you have the distinct impression of having stepped across a threshold into another, higher world. Lord Kenneth Clark, the great twentieth-century art historian, said that when the light pours through the colored glass of the Sainte-Chapelle, it sets up a kind of vibration in the air, an electrical charge. It is, if you will, the artistic representation of the electric meeting of two spirits, human and divine. It is what a human heart, elevated to and by God, looks like: transfigured, luminous, radiantly beautiful.

This elevation through prayer is, ultimately, from God. One of the most fundamental truths in the Bible is that the spiritual life is not primarily our quest for God, but rather God's quest for us. Therefore, as Herbert Mc-Cabe argued so clearly, whatever is good, true, and beautiful in our prayer is God already praying, as it were, in us. Karl Rahner defined prayer as God's self-communication, given in grace, and accepted in freedom. And a contemporary commentator on St. John of the Cross, who is maybe the greatest master of prayer in the Catholic tradition, said that God is like a helicopter, and prayer is a bit like clearing the ground in order to make the landing of the helicopter easier. It is not as though God is off in the distance waiting for us to come crawling to him; no, God is waiting to come and inhabit our hearts. The problem is that the landing ground is all cluttered. Prayer on this reading is clearing out all those attachments, preoccupations, and addictions that prevent God from fully landing in our hearts.

The Lord says—and all of Christian spirituality follows from it in a way—"You did not choose me but I chose you" (John 15:16). God wants to come into our lives, and prayer is an opening of the door, a clearing of the ground, to let him come. Fr. Paul Murray, quoting from the Dominican writer William Peraldus, puts it this way: "Prayer is such an easy job!" It is like breathing: we were born for prayer. To open the door to Christ is the easiest thing of all.

2

A Conversation Between Friends

PERHAPS THE BEST IMAGE for prayer is a conversation between friends. What should this ongoing conversation, this deepening friendship, look like? Let me offer four suggestions.

First, the most important thing with regard to any friendship is that we *take the time*. Thomas Merton, the greatest spiritual teacher of the twentieth century, was once asked, "What is the best thing I can do to improve my prayer life?" His simple answer: "Take the time." If you claimed that a certain person was your best friend but had to admit you spend almost no time with him, people would laugh at you. But a lot of people will say that God is the most important person in their life and yet spend next to no time speaking or listening to him. Don't say blithely, "I find God in all things." Reserve time for God—both when you feel like it and when you don't. Perhaps it is in the morning; perhaps it's late at night. Maybe it's in the car (which can be a very good place to pray—your own little monastic cell); maybe it's an hour or even a half hour before the Blessed Sacrament. In a way, it doesn't matter, as long as it is substantial and intentional time with God. Under this rubric, we might even speak of prayer as *wasting* time with God.

When you speak to God during this time of prayer, you also must *speak with honesty*. What would happen to a human relationship in which honesty did not hold sway? It would quickly grow cold and superficial. How do you feel when a friend is keeping important things from you, dissembling, or covering up? Far too often in prayer, we tell God what we think he wants to hear, presenting ourselves as pious; things that seem messy, dirty, or unkempt in our lives, we sweep under the carpet.

But this is so much nonsense! Take a good, prayerful look at Psalm 139 sometime: "O LORD, you have searched me and known me" (Ps. 139:1). Tell the Lord what's happening in your life—the good, the bad, and the ugly. Tell him what's frightening you and what's depressing you. Confess your sins before him in the manner of David and Peter, and tell him how guilty you feel when you sin. There is a lot of talk of tears in the Bible; in fact, the saints speak of the "gift of tears." If anything shows that you're not just going through the motions, this is it.

Speak your anger to him—especially your anger *at* him. I love the story of a woman whose husband was in the hospital for many months, dying of a terrible illness. There was a statue of the Blessed Mother outside of the hospital, and one day, the wife became so frustrated that, upon leaving the hospital, she began to pick up rocks and dirt and throw them at the statue. Security ran out to stop her, but one of the sisters held them back, saying, "No—don't stop her. She's praying." Consider the number of figures in the Bible who regularly expressed this sort of frustration, confusion, and anger to God: the Psalmist, Abraham, Moses, Jeremiah, and above all, Job.

Relatedly, when you pray, you must also *listen with attention*. Obviously, a conversation between friends cannot be a one-way street. If all you ever did was talk to a friend, he wouldn't be your friend very long. Far too often, we think of prayer as simply talking to God. It is indeed, but it is also taking the time to listen to him—both breathing out and breathing in.

Some people in our tradition have heard the voice of God in a physical or quasi-physical way—we could cite the many examples from the Scriptures and the great tradition, such as Mother Teresa's experience of hearing the voice of Jesus—but God speaks this clearly and unambiguously only very rarely indeed. Normally, God delights in speaking indirectly. It might be through reading the Scriptures or listening to a liturgical song; it might be in Eucharistic Adoration or during the Mass. Feelings of consolation or desolation, a sense of the whole body relaxing and finding peace, the arrival of an insight about a particular problem or of a memory of someone from whom we've grown distant—all of these can be carriers of the divine word, routes by which God communicates with us, sometimes with an extraordinary power and clarity, from beyond ourselves.

Sometimes, in prayer, we can even legitimately imagine what God would say to us in response to a question or a communication. This can be dangerous, of course, insofar as it begins to resemble a psychological projection. But based on our knowledge of God from the Bible and the tradition, this imaginative exercise can be another way of discerning the voice of God.

Finally, one of the most important though under-rated features of prayer is *silence*. When Mother Teresa spoke of prayer, the first thing she mentioned was silence: "The fruit of silence is prayer; the fruit of prayer is faith; the fruit of faith is love; the fruit of love is service; the fruit of service is peace." We have a very noisy culture; we are constantly stimulating ourselves with words and ideas, talking and listening to each other all the time. Do we sit in silence, allowing God to speak in that space?

Think here of the prophet Elijah in 1 Kings, who, on Mount Horeb, does not hear God in the wind, the earthquake, or the fire, but rather in "a sound of sheer silence" (1 Kings 19:12). So it still is. How can you hear the voice of God unless you become silent? When the noises subside, the Voice can be heard. Think, too, of how many religious orders—the Carthusian order founded by St. Bruno, for example—are predicated upon this discipline. Most of us can't be Carthusians, but we can learn a lot from their attitude of radical devotion to silence.

Thomas Aquinas speaks of the two basic moves of the will: to seek the absent good and to savor the present good, resting in it in a kind of silence. We're rather skilled at the first but not the second: once we have the good, we restlessly go on to something else. When you have the good of God, a silent savoring of that good is key; that, too, is part of prayer. Notice how old friends can spend a good amount of time together without speaking—and the better their friendship, the longer and more comfortable their silence.

So, when it comes to prayer, take the time; speak with honestly; listen with attention; and enter into silence. Your friendship with God depends on it!

3

The Christian Difference

THOUGH PRAYER CAN BE FOUND in all the great religious traditions, there is something unique about Christian prayer—namely, that we address God as our Father. If Christians were to speak to God in an undifferentiated way, then we would not be praying in a manner different than the way a pious Jew, Muslim, or general monotheist would pray, petitioning, adoring, or begging God from "outside." The Christian difference is that the one God has revealed himself in three persons—the Father, the Son, and the Holy Spirit—and that the Father has sent his Son into our humanity, and indeed, all the way down into sin and death. Thus, when we pray, the Son stands *beside* us, so to speak, with his arm around our shoulder, helping us to pray to the Father *in* the Holy Spirit—the very love that connects Father and Son. In an extraordinary privilege, Christians have been drawn into these dynamics of the inner life of God; he has opened up the Trinitarian life and now includes us in it.

This is why, whenever we pray as Christians, we begin with the sign of the cross: "In the name of the Father, and of the Son, and of the Holy Spirit." This is the distinctive metaphysical space into which Christians enter when we pray, and it makes a world of difference. We are not addressing God from some external standpoint; we are not approaching the divine simply as a seeker or supplicant or penitent. We are *in* the divine life, speaking to the Father, through the Son, and in the Holy Spirit. It has been said that Christian prayer is listening intently as the Father and the Son speak about you. It is this peculiar intimacy—praying in God and not just to him—that gives the Christian practice of prayer its unique texture.

This does not mean, of course, that the Christian cannot also pray to Jesus or to the Holy Spirit. God is one in essence—the Father, Son, and Spirit share the same nature—and the theological tradition signals this by speaking of the "circumincession" of the three persons. You never have the Father without the Son and the Spirit, the Spirit without the Father and the Son, or the Son without the Father and the Spirit; they are always together. Thus, a Christian can also pray, "Lord Jesus, help me," because the Father and the Spirit are co-implicated in that petition; or they can pray, "Come, Holy Spirit," because if they invoke the Spirit, they invoke, necessarily, the Father and the Son too. But the fundamental move, reflected in our liturgical prayers, is praying *to* the Father, *with* the Son, *in* the unity of the Holy Spirit.

However we pray, as Christians we pray *for one another*. If the essence of prayer is resting in God's creative love, then whenever we pray, we are linked, willy-nilly, to everyone and everything else in the cosmos. In the divine still point, we find the ground from which all things proceed and by which they are sustained. And thus, the very act of prayer is necessarily communal and corporate.

Charles Williams took as the elemental principle of the Christian life the play of co-inherence—that is to say, existing in and for the other. Just as the Father gives himself away totally in the Son and the Son returns the favor by existing totally for the Father, so all creation is, at its best, marked by this metaphysics of co-implication, co-involvement.

There is a hint of co-inherence in the radical interdependency of the things of nature, but it is more apparent in the complex and dramatic interpenetrations of human psyches, bodies, and souls. I am able, in love, to place my mind in your mind and to project my will into yours in such a way as to bear your burdens. When Christians speak of praying for one another or, even more radically, of suffering on behalf of one another, they are assuming this ontology of co-inherence. Of course, its greatest archetype (after the Trinity itself) is the substitutionary sacrifice of Christ on the cross, whereby Jesus truly suffered *for* the world, his pain literally taking away the pain of a sinful world. This sort of language becomes coherent only in light of the unifying power of life in Christ.

4

The Disorienting Quality of Real Prayer

ONE OF THE MOST IMPRESSIVE literary figures of the twentieth century was the Irish-British writer Iris Murdoch. A careful examination of Murdoch's fiction and nonfiction reveals her consistently dark take on human nature. Left to our own devices, we are, she thinks, self-absorbed, violent, and all too willing to draw the whole world into the narrow confines of our egotism. In this conviction, of course, she is not far from the classical Christian doctrine of original sin. What we require, she concludes, are spiritual exercises that serve to break us out of the prison of our self-absorption; and since we are so ensconced in the pattern of self-reference, these must be rather shocking reversals of the status quo. We need the Good—in one form or another—to burst through the carapace of our fearful self-regard. Her insights about these spiritual exercises illuminate for us the disorienting quality of authentic prayer.

A first such exercise, Murdoch suggests, is the learning of a foreign language. Playing at another language can be a mildly diverting experience, and it can convince one that the language can be used after the manner of a game. But when one is really compelled to learn a language well, for the sake of survival or success, one quickly discovers just how unyielding, how demanding, and how unforgiving that language can be. French doesn't care whether you learn its nuances, its vocabulary, or its sometimes-irrational spellings; German couldn't care less whether or not you appreciate its (to English-speakers) confounding word order; Greek is not the least bit put out if you cannot master its alphabet; and Latin is utterly indifferent to your struggles with its endings and cases. All of these linguistic systems are, in their objectivity, order, confusion, and beauty, massively there, and they compel the one who would dare to learn them to submit.

The demanding "there-ness" of the French language was symbolized for me one day soon after I had arrived in Paris for my doctoral studies. I was with some friends in a crowded restaurant at the height of the dinner rush when a stereotypically haughty and impatient waiter came to take our order. When he turned his imperious gaze toward me and uttered a curt *Oui?* I promptly forgot all of my carefully memorized restaurant vocabulary and every one of my past participles, and devolved before his eyes into a muttering, incoherent child. His reaction to my plight? He turned and walked away.

A second spiritual exercise recommended by Iris Murdoch for the disciplining of the ego is a confrontation with a true work of art. Second-rate art is designed primarily to please. Comfortable, familiar, likable, it presents no particular challenge to the sensibilities of the one who takes it in. For example, the music heard in an elevator or a doctor's waiting room is meant simply to provide a mild distraction or a feeling of calm in the listener; and the paintings that hang in most hotel rooms or corporate lobbies are intended to provide low-level entertainment. These works fit predictably into universally recognized canons of appropriateness and, as such, are forgotten almost as soon as they are taken in.

But a great and true work of art does not aim to please. Rather, it presents itself in its integrity on its own terms, remaining fundamentally indifferent to the reaction of the viewer or listener. In a scene from his autobiographical masterpiece, *A Portrait of the Artist as a Young Man*, James Joyce brilliantly displays the dynamics of confronting the truly beautiful. Stephen Dedalus (Joyce's fictional alter ego) is pacing listlessly on the strand outside of Dublin when he spies, standing out in the surf, a woman of surpassing beauty. He is stopped in his tracks—in the state of aesthetic arrest—and takes the woman in. She turns to him at one point and "quietly suffered his gaze" before turning back to look out at the open sea. Indifferent to his feelings or reactions, she allows him to watch. Finally, changed utterly by this encounter, Stephen cries out, "Heavenly God!" and resolves from that moment on to become an artist, a reporter of such epiphanies of the beautiful. The lovely girl standing just off the strand did not so much please Stephen Dedalus as change him, drawing him effectively out of his morose self-regard and giving him his vocation. Hans Urs von Balthasar observes, in a very similar vein, that the beautiful elects the observer and then sends him on mission to announce what he has seen.

Not many years ago, *Rolling Stone* magazine asked

a number of prominent popular musicians to name the song that first "rocked their world." Some of the responses were relatively banal, but the vast majority of them had a Joycean resonance: the respondents knew instinctively the difference between songs (however great) that had merely pleased them and songs that had shaken them out of their complacency and rearranged their vision of things. This kind of aesthetic encounter is the spiritual exercise that Murdoch is speaking of.

It is against this Murdochian background that I would like to consider the familiar Gospel story of the Pharisee and the publican (Luke 18:9–14) and what it tells us about real prayer. Jesus tells of a Pharisee who, "standing by himself, was praying thus, 'God, I thank you that I am not like other people: thieves, rogues, adulterers, or even like this tax collector.'" This is, Jesus suggests, a fraudulent, wholly inadequate prayer precisely because it simply confirms the man in his self-regard. The words are, obviously enough, just elaborate self-congratulation, but even the Pharisee's body language gives him away: he takes up his position, standing with a confidence bordering on arrogance in the presence of God. The prayer itself confirms the Pharisee's world. Like a second-rate work of art, or like the tourist's language spoken by the dilettante, it functions simply to please. And the god to which he prays is, necessarily, a false god, an idol, since it allows itself to be positioned by the ego-driven needs of the Pharisee.

But then Jesus invites us to meditate upon the publican's prayer. First, his stance is telling: "But the tax collector, standing far off, would not even look up to heaven." This man realizes that he is in the presence of a power that he cannot even in principle manipulate or control; and he signals with his body, accordingly, that he is positioned by this higher authority. Then, "beating his breast," he speaks with a simple eloquence: "God, be merciful to me, a sinner!" Though it is articulate speech, proceeding from the mind and will of the publican, it is not language that confirms the independence and power of the speaker—just the contrary. It is more of a cry or a groan, an acknowledgment that he needs to receive something: this mysterious mercy for which he begs.

In the first prayer, god is the principal member of the audience arrayed before the ego of the Pharisee. But in this second prayer, God is the principal actor, and the publican is the audience awaiting a performance the contours of which he cannot fully foresee. And therefore, the publican's prayer is the kind of spiritual exercise of which Iris Murdoch speaks. It is akin to the experience of being mastered by the French language, or by Picasso's *Guernica*, or by Bernini's *Ecstasy of Saint Teresa*.

Some of the most powerful prayers are simple, unadorned, even blunt. They have the essential virtue of knocking the ego off of its pedestal and rocking the world of the one who utters them. In this, they both open the sinner to transformation and honor the true God.

5

Transfigured Prayer

WHAT IS IT ABOUT THE STORY of the Transfiguration that is just so compelling? It is like a play or a movie that we can watch over and over again and still derive new insights. We can never fully exhaust its meaning. Indeed, the Transfiguration can serve as an occasion to reflect on the nature of prayer.

In Luke's version (9:28–36), we first hear that Jesus took Peter, James, and John with him "up on the mountain to pray." Now, mountains are standard biblical places of encounter with God, who was imagined as living in the sky. Thus, the higher you go, the closer you come to God. We don't have to literalize this, but we should unpack its symbolic sense. In order to commune with God, you have to step out of your everyday, workaday world. The mountain symbolizes transcendence, otherness, the realm of God. Those who say "I pray on the go" or "My work is my prayer" are not really people of prayer.

Like Christ and the Apostles, you have to step away—step up, if you want—from the ordinary routine in order to commune with God. What is your mountain, your place of encounter? It could be before the Blessed

Sacrament or in the hushed darkness of a church; it could be a special room in your house or a corner of the natural world—even a literal mountain. But it has to be someplace where you have stepped away from your ordinary business.

We hear next that "while he was praying, the appearance of his face changed, and his clothes became dazzling white." The reference here—no first-century Jew would have missed it—is to Moses, whose face was transfigured after he communed with God on Mount Sinai. But the luminosity is meant in general to signal the invasion of God. In the depths of prayer, when you have achieved a communion with the Lord, the light of God's presence is kindled deep inside of you, at the very core of your existence, and then it begins to radiate out through the whole of your being. This is why it is so important that Luke mentions the clothing of Jesus becoming dazzling white. Clothes evoke one's contact with the outside world. The God discovered in prayer should radiate out through you to the world so that you might become a source of illumination.

Stay for a moment with the image of light. Light is that by which we see and understand. Who are the people who become sources of light to the world? Those who are rooted in prayer. They become beacons by which people around them see and understand their world more completely. We often depict the saints with haloes, with lights around them, which is making the same point: the saints are those who are so grounded in God that they become like torches or lanterns to others around them. You've probably had the experience of being with somebody who just seems to shed light in every direction. When you're with that person, you not only feel better and more at peace; you actually come to understand things more clearly. That person is a source of light—which means, I can almost guarantee you, a person of prayer.

Now, when Jesus was transfigured, "suddenly they saw two men, Moses and Elijah, talking to him." In this beautiful image, Jesus is communing with the great prophet, Elijah, and the great representative of the Law, Moses. When you pray, when you step out of the ordinary world of space and time, you enter into the properly eternal realm of God. And this means that you come into contact with the past and the future. You establish contact with what the Church calls "the communion of saints"—all those friends of God up and down the centuries. That's why we speak of invoking the saints—even saints who lived and died long ago—speaking with them, seeking their help and intercession. This is not just pious talk; it is grounded in this metaphysics of eternity.

But what precisely are Jesus, Moses, and Elijah talking about? "His departure [*exodos*], which he was about to accomplish at Jerusalem." We notice, first of all, the wonderful thematic connection between the exodus that Moses led—a journey from slavery to freedom—and the exodus that Jesus would accomplish on the cross: a journey from sin and death to resurrection. In both cases, it is a great work of liberation and of life-giving love—and that is the key. The fruit of prayer in the biblical tradition is always action on behalf of the world. We are, essentially, a mission religion. Even the highest moments of mystical union are meant, in the end, to conduce to doing God's work in the world, to becoming a conduit of the divine grace. Why do you pray? To commune with God, to commune with the saints, but finally, to become a vehicle of God's grace. Prayer awakens you to your duty and responsibility to the world. We have mystics, poets, and contemplatives galore in our tradition—just think of Bernard, John of the Cross, Teresa of Avila, Meister Eckhart, Thomas Merton—but they all saw this essential link between prayer and action.

This is why Peter's line is so important: "Master, it is good for us to be here; let us make three dwellings, one for you, one for Moses, and one for Elijah"—not knowing, as Luke points out immediately, what he was saying. When you're in prayer, lifted up outside of the realm of ordinary experience and into the realm of God's eternity, you don't quite know where you are or what to say. Peter seems lost here, and that's appropriate when you're in this "cloud of unknowing," as one of the great mystics called it. But the point of prayer is not to stay on the mountain. It is not to cling to mystical experience, however wonderful. It is to become so radiant with the divine life that you can share it with the world. You have to come back down the mountain and resume the hard work of following Jesus. And this is why the voice from the cloud, once it identified Jesus, specified, "Listen to him!" In other words, don't just admire him; don't simply worship him from a distance; rather, do what he tells you. Come back down the mountain.

Part II

Principles of Prayer

6

The Four Rules of Prayer

HOW SHOULD WE PRAY? What makes prayer efficacious? Why does it seem that some prayers are answered and others are not? How does prayer "work"? These are questions that come not simply from theoreticians of religion but from religious people, from ordinary believers. Studies indicate that we are a nation of pray-ers, yet we struggle rather mightily with the mechanics, meaning, and practicalities of prayer.

I would like to share four "rules" of prayer. These are not the elements of an airtight formula ("Follow these and your prayer will be answered"), but rather powerful and consistent indications regarding the practice of prayer, coming from the biblical texts and refined by the great tradition.

Rule one: you must pray with faith. Have you noticed how, in Matthew's Gospel, Jesus says to two blind men before he works a miracle, "Do you believe that I am able to do this?" (Matt. 9:28). Matthew also tells us that, on one occasion, Jesus was unable to perform many healings in a given place because he met with so little faith among the people there (Matt. 13:58). And Mark reports this word of the Lord: "Truly I tell you, if you say to this mountain, 'Be taken up and thrown into the sea,' and if you do not doubt in your heart, but believe that what you say will come to pass, it will be done for you" (Mark 11:23). After Bartimaeus receives his sight, Jesus says to him, "Go; your faith has made you well" (Mark 10:52). There are many Christians today, working in the healing ministries, who seem able, through the simplicity and integrity of their trust, to produce miraculous effects after the manner of Jesus himself.

How can we explain this correlation between faith and the answering of prayer? Again, we should never think of this in an automatic way, since we are always dealing with the freedom and sovereignty of God. Nevertheless, we might suggest the following connection. God's grace and loving-kindness are neither manipulative nor domineering; instead, they require, by God's design, the conduit of a receptive freedom in order to be realized in our lives. It is a commonplace of Catholic theology that God is always pleased to work in cooperation with our powers of will and mind. Faith, therefore, is this conduit, this open door; it is a signal, coming from the depths of our existence, that we want to cooperate with grace. We might, therefore, follow the extraordinary advice that Jesus offers in the eleventh chapter of Mark's Gospel: "So I tell you, whatever you ask for in prayer, believe that you have received it, and it will be yours" (Mark 11:24). In other words, let your faith be so pure and strong that you easily believe that you already have what you have asked God to give you—and you may find that you do indeed receive it.

A second rule of prayer is this: if you want your

prayer answered, forgive. There is an exhortation of the Lord, found in the Gospel of Matthew, that, over the centuries, has conditioned the liturgical practice of the Church: "So when you are offering your gift at the altar, if you remember that your brother or sister has something against you, leave your gift there before the altar and go; first be reconciled to your brother or sister, and then come and offer your gift" (Matt. 5:23–24). And in that same eleventh chapter of Mark that we considered above, there is this piece of blunt advice: "Whenever you stand praying, forgive, if you have anything against anyone; so that your Father in heaven may also forgive you your trespasses" (Mark 11:25). In both cases, Jesus seems to imply, if not a strict causal connection, at least a correspondence between answered prayer and the reconciliation of differences. It appears as though effective prayer is simply incompatible with the nursing of grudges and the bearing of resentments.

Why should this be the case? Again, it is impossible to respond with anything like demonstrable certitude, but we might suggest that it has something to do with the nature of God. When one prays, one is asking, essentially, for some participation in the life of God. But God is love. Therefore, to remain in an act or attitude that contradicts love would, it seems, place an obstacle in the way of grace. If some decent request of yours is being stubbornly refused, look at the quality of your relationships and see if there is not something there that is repugnant to the nature of the God you are petitioning.

A third rule of prayer, on display throughout the biblical witness, is to pray with perseverance. We see this in that wonderful Genesis account of Abraham dickering with God over the destruction of Sodom: "Suppose there are fifty righteous within the city. . . . Suppose forty are found there. . . . Suppose ten are found there" (Gen. 18:24, 29, 32). With a sort of sacred chutzpah, Abraham stands in the presence of God and stubbornly, persistently asks for what he wants. And in one of Jesus' parables, we hear of a man who knocks at his neighbor's door only to be told that the neighbor and his wife are in bed and cannot be bothered. He knocks again and again, until finally, in exasperation, the neighbor relents and gives the petitioner what he seeks. This story is, of course, followed by Jesus' unambiguous teaching: "Ask, and it will be given you; search, and you will find; knock, and the door will be opened for you" (Luke 11:9).

It appears as though one reason we don't receive what we want through prayer is that we give up far too easily. Precisely when we are refused, our ardor should grow and our desire should increase so as to receive the fullness of what God desires for us. This process is short-circuited when, in our frustration at not being answered promptly, we cease to ask.

A fourth and final rule of prayer, embodied, like rule two, in the liturgical tradition of the Christian churches, is this: pray in Jesus' name. The ground for this rule is in the explicit statement of Christ: "I will do whatever you ask in my name, so that the Father may be glorified in the Son. If in my name you ask me for anything, I will do it" (John 14:13-14). When we pray in the name of Jesus, we are relying on his intimacy with the Father, trusting that the Father will listen to his Son who pleads on our behalf. In the Letter to the Hebrews, we hear that Jesus, like us in all things but sin, a fellow sufferer with us, has entered as our advocate into the heavenly court.

Risking a crude comparison, it is as though Jesus is our man in city hall, a representative for us in the place of ultimate power. Just as a lowly petitioner in Washington might get his senator's attention by dropping the name of an influential acquaintance, so we Christians confidently mention the name of Jesus while petitioning at the throne of the Father. Mind you, this analogy is limited: the Father must not be construed as a reluctant and distracted executive, annoyed by the petty appeals of his constituents mediated by a persistent lobbyist. For the author of the Letter to the Hebrews, Jesus has become our advocate precisely because the Father wanted him to assume this role for us; and therefore, presumably, the Father delights in hearing us call upon him through his Son.

There is another dimension to this rule. Invoking the name of Jesus is an effective way to monitor the quality and to shape the content of our prayer. When we pray "through Christ our Lord," we are assuming the stance and attitude of Jesus, aligning ourselves to him, compelling ourselves to desire what he desires. Accordingly, it is altogether consistent to pray in the name of Jesus for peace, for justice, for the forgiveness of our enemies, for greater faith, or for the health of those we love. Those are all goods that Jesus would want. But how anomalous it would be to pray for vengeance against our enemies in Jesus' name or for a Maserati through Christ our Lord!

Therefore, follow the rules of prayer: pray with faith; pray in conjunction with acts of forgiveness; pray with persistence; and pray in the name of Jesus.

7

Why We Should Address
Jesus as Thou

ON THE FINAL MORNING of one November meeting of the United States Conference of Catholic Bishops, we were treated to a fine sermon by Archbishop J. Peter Sartain. What particularly struck me in his homily was a reference to the great St. Catherine of Siena. One of the most remarkable things about that remarkable woman was the intimacy that she regularly experienced with Mary, the saints, and the Lord Jesus himself. Archbishop Sartain relayed a story reported by Catherine's spiritual director, Raymond of Capua. According to Raymond, Catherine would often recite the Divine Office while walking along a cloister in the company of Jesus, mystically visible to the saint. When she came to the conclusion of a Psalm, she would, according to liturgical custom, speak the words of the Glory Be, but her version was as follows: "Glory be to the Father, and to Thee, and to the Holy Ghost!" For her, Christ was not a distant figure, and prayer was not an abstract exercise. Rather, the Lord was at her side, and prayer was a conversation between friends.

Archbishop Sartain invited us to muse on Catherine's use of the intimate form of the pronoun, in her Latin, *tibi* (to you), and rightly rendered in English as "to Thee." As is the case with many other languages, Latin distinguishes between more formal and more informal use of the second person pronoun, and it is the familiar *tu* that Catherine employs when speaking to Jesus. It is an oddity of the evolution of spoken English that, today, "thou, thine, thy, and thee" seem more rarified, more regal and distant, when in fact, just the contrary was the case up until fairly modern times. These were the words used to address family members, children, and intimate friends, in contradistinction to the more formal "you" and "yours." How wonderful, Archbishop Sartain reminded us, that this intimate usage is preserved in some of our most beloved prayers. We say, "Our Father, who art in heaven, hallowed be *thy* name; *thy* kingdom come, *thy* will be done . . ." And we pray, "Hail Mary, full of grace, the Lord is with *thee*. Blessed art *thou* among women and blessed is the fruit of *thy* womb, Jesus." Again, I realize that to our ears, this language sounds less rather than more intimate, but it is in fact meant to convey the same easy familiarity with the Father and the Blessed Mother that Catherine of Siena enjoyed with Christ.

And all of this signals something of crucial significance regarding the nature of biblical Christianity. Many mysticisms and philosophies of the ancient world—Platonism, Neoplatonism, and Gnosticism come readily to mind—indeed spoke of God or the sacred, but they meant a force or a value or an ontological source, impersonal and at an infinite remove from the world of ordinary experience. These ancient schools find an echo, moreover, in many modern and contemporary theologies. Think of the Deism popular in the eighteenth century and so influential on the founders of the United States; or think of Schleiermacher's and Emerson's pantheist mysticisms in the nineteenth century; or consider even the New Age philosophy of our time. All of these would speak of a "divine" principle or power, but one would never dream of addressing such a force as "thou" or of engaging with it in intimate conversation.

Then there is the Bible. The Scriptures obviously present God as overwhelming, transcendent, uncontrollable, inscrutable, the Creator of the heavens and the earth, but they insist that this sublime and frightening power is a person who deigns to speak to us, to guide us, and to invite us into his life. They even make bold to speak of the awesome God "pitching his tent among us" (see John 1:14), becoming one of us, taking to himself our frail humanity. And this implies that we can speak to God as we speak to an intimate colleague. Conversing with his disciples the night before he died, Jesus said, "I do not call you servants any longer . . . but I have called you friends" (John 15:15), and in making that utterance, he turned all of religious philosophy and mysticism on its head.

I believe that one of the major problems we have in evangelizing our culture is that many Christians don't walk with Jesus personally. Evangelization is not, finally, a sharing of ideas—though this can be very important at the level of pre-evangelization or clearing the ground— but rather the sharing of a relationship. But as the old adage has it, "*Nemo dat quod non habet*" (No one gives what he doesn't have). If we don't speak to Jesus as "thou," we won't draw others into a real *friendship* with him, and the establishment of that friendship is the goal, the *terminus ad quem*, of real evangelizing.

8

The Prayers of the Saints

ONCE, WHILE WORKING at my computer in Santa Barbara, I encountered a confounding problem and decided to call Brandon Vogt, who is not only the excellent Senior Publishing Director at Word on Fire but also a trained engineer and tech whiz. After trying in vain to talk me through the problem, Brandon said, "Look, let me just take over your screen." And with that, he pressed some buttons in Atlanta, where he was attending a conference, and then commenced to move my cursor around the screen, click on all the right settings, and resolve the difficulty.

Though I had seen him do this before, I was, once again, impressed by this long-distance maneuver. Displaying my utter lack of scientific expertise, I asked, "Now, Brandon, is this being done through the phone lines or is outer space involved?" I'm sure he was suppressing a laugh, but he patiently explained that when we send data over the internet, the data is broken down into invisible electromagnetic waves, which are then passed through miles and miles of cables, telephone lines, and sometimes satellites. What's remarkable, he explained, is how the same cables and satellites handle information from billions of computers, phones, and other devices *simultaneously*.

At this point in the conversation, Brandon remarked, "You know, I've often thought it analogous to the communion of saints." "You'll have to unpack that for me," I said. "Well," he replied, "people always seem puzzled that the saints in heaven can hear and answer millions of prayers without being omnipotent; and yet, something similar is happening all the time through our technology. Each second, we send and receive an unfathomable amount of data through our cables and satellites, yet they handle it. The relatively small number of intercessions we pray each day pales in comparison."

One of the forms of Catholic prayer is an invocation of those in the heavenly realm. Every time we say the Hail Mary, for instance, we are confident that Mary, the Queen of Heaven, hears that prayer and engages us. Every time we call upon one of the saints, we are convinced that he or she takes in what we say and can, in point of fact, respond to us with information or inspiration. Indeed, we believe that our prayer can prompt the saints to act on our behalf, effecting real change in the world. I realize how counterintuitive this can all seem to most moderns. In our more "realistic" moments, we feel that the dead are just gone, that they can't possibly hear us. Or maybe we think that, if they still exist, they are far away, infinitely removed from the things of this world. And how, we wonder, could the Blessed Mother possibly "hear" every single Hail Mary that goes up to her every day from across the globe? Isn't all of this just wishful thinking, so much prescientific mumbo jumbo?

Well, remember Brandon's insight. A machine of our contrivance is capable of receiving and transmitting extraordinary amounts of information simultaneously to and from numberless locales. How much more thoroughly and powerfully, therefore, can an intelligence at a higher pitch of reality, in a qualitatively different dimensional system, receive and transmit information? The faith of the Church is that those who are in the heavenly realm participate more intensely in the infinite intelligence of God, that intelligence which embraces all of space and all of time. Can a saint, therefore, receive and send a staggering amount of information? Why not? But can a saint exert a causal influence on the physical dimension? Can they actually *do* something for us? We mustn't think of the spiritual as simply "other" than the material, as though the two could never interact. Rather, the spiritual contains the physical in the measure that it subsists at an elevated, more ontologically complete, level of existence. Representing the medieval consensus, Thomas Aquinas said that the soul is in the body "not as contained by it, but as containing it." Instead of being a "ghost in the machine," as many modern philosophers speculated, the soul, on Aquinas' reading, is *inclusive* of the body. It can move matter, for it is greater than matter. And so the saints, from their heavenly place, can indeed influence, impact, and shape the material world.

Perhaps a last point of comparison would be in order. The satellites that facilitate so much of our world's communication are entirely out of sight. We don't, in the ordinary sense of the term, interact with them at all as we do with other persons and objects. And yet, from their celestial abode, they massively affect and aid us. In one of the prefaces for saints in the Roman Missal, we find this language: "You, eternal shepherd, do not desert your flock, but through the blessed Apostles, watch over it and protect it." We don't deal with the denizens of heaven as we do with those of earth, but yet they listen to us, speak to us, and influence us constantly.

So next time you receive some instruction on your GPS or make a call on your iPhone, think of the communion of saints.

Part III

Types of Prayer

Contrition and Cleansing the Temple

ONE OF THE GREAT FORMS of prayer is "contrition"—
literally, "crushing," from *contritio*. In the hard, grinding
work of contrition, the sinner feels the pain that his sin
has caused himself and others: "The sacrifice acceptable
to God is a broken spirit; a broken and contrite heart,
O God, you will not despise" (Ps. 51:17). This involves,
of course, a stark confrontation with the reality of sin;
we must see ourselves with clarity and uncompromising
honesty. And one of the best ways into this searching
moral inventory is by attending to the account of the Ten
Commandments (Exod. 20:1-17).

The first three commandments have to do with the
question of one's fundamental spiritual orientation. And
so we need to hear the very first commandment: "I am
the LORD your God . . . you shall have no other gods before me." There is nothing more fundamental. Everyone
worships something or someone; everyone has an ultimate concern. Who or what, precisely, is the object of
your worship? What do you hold to be spiritually basic?
If we're honest, a lot of us would say something like sex,
money, power, status—or, to sum all of this up, our own

egos. The most basic intuition of the Bible is that having an ultimate concern other than God leads to disaster, to a falling apart of the self.

Relatedly, "You shall not make wrongful use of the name of the LORD your God." It is one thing to claim that God is the ultimate good in your life; it is quite another to instantiate it through speech. Do you speak of God in a derogatory or denigrating way? This leads, rather quickly, to a denigration of God and to a coarsening of the soul.

The third commandment is even more telling: "Remember the sabbath day, and keep it holy." One must instantiate one's commitment to God through definite acts of worship; otherwise, that commitment becomes an abstraction and then an irrelevancy. Worship cannot be simply an interior disposition; it must express itself through action. There is no place for the attitude of "I'm all right with God; I just have no time for going to Mass" or "I get nothing out of the Mass." Do you meet your obligation to concretize your worship on Sundays and Holy Days?

Following from this basic form of worship, there comes a whole series of commandments dealing with our relations to other people. To love God is to love everyone whom God loves; so the love of God spills over into love of neighbor. First, "Honor your father and your mother." Most biblical commentators have seen this as a command to attend to the obligations of one's family, the people closest to you. If you claim to be a person of love but fail to honor your parents, your siblings, and your children, something is seriously off; and if things are off there, they are probably off everywhere else. What is the quality of your relationship with those who are nearest to you?

"You shall not murder." I suppose that very few murderers are reading this book right now. Nevertheless, killing is not a minor problem in our world. From the tens of millions of unborn children killed since *Roe v. Wade* to the almost casual murder of young people on the streets of our cities, killing is everywhere. A basic biblical intuition is that God is the Lord and giver of life. We have no business, except in the case of self-defense and just war, interfering with that prerogative. But broaden the commandment out a bit: What is the role that violence plays in your life? What is the quality of your temper? Have you effectively killed people—that is to say, rendered them lifeless? Do you enhance the lives of those around you, or are people less alive after they've been with you?

"You shall not commit adultery." Does anyone doubt that the violation of the marriage vow is a major problem in our society? Or that marriage itself is in serious trouble in our world? The family is the fundamental building block of society, and thus, when the family goes bad, the whole society goes bad. But again, broaden the commandment out: Is your sex life self-indulgent and for the sake of your own pleasure? Do you lust after others, using them for your own sexual satisfaction? Do you practice forms of sex that fall outside of its proper setting in marriage—a union of one man and one woman in life-long fidelity and openness to children? The Bible is not obsessed with sex, but it does recognize the importance of sexuality in the moral sphere. Much of our popular culture wants to teach us that sex is basically amoral—a matter, finally, of indifference. As long as you're not hurting anyone, anything goes. But sex, like everything else in us, is meant to serve love, to become a gift.

"You shall not steal." There is something uniquely depressing and violating about being robbed. It is a particularly awful violation of one's rights and personhood. Do you steal others' property, even very small things or little amounts of money? Do you perhaps steal on a grand scale? How dispiriting corporate scandals are. White collar crime, negotiated through computers, is no less a crime. Have you made restitution after stealing something?

"You shall not bear false witness against your neighbor." How we love tearing each other down! It is a function of the ego's need to be superior, to feel protected. Our favorite indoor pastime is critiquing others. What is the quality of your speech? How much time do you spend inveighing against your neighbor, even making things up to make him look bad? How much time do you spend scapegoating, blaming, and accusing others? One of my professors at Mundelein, Jack Shea, offered this admonition: Say all you want in criticism of another, as long as you are willing to commit yourself to helping the person deal with the problem you have named.

"You shall not covet your neighbor's house; you shall not covet your neighbor's wife." The Catholic anthropologist René Girard constructed a complex theory that hinges on this tendency to desire what our neighbor has. Desire is mimetic: we want something not because of its intrinsic merits but because someone else wants it. Just watch little children at play, advertising techniques, or romantic relationships. This competitive coveting leads, Girard argues, to most of the conflicts that bedevil human societies. Do you play these games of conflict? Do you fuss about what other people have and what other people desire?

In the Gospels, we hear how Jesus entered the great temple in Jerusalem and began to turn over the tables of the moneychangers, tearing the place apart. From the earliest days, Christian writers and spiritual teachers saw the temple as symbolic of the human person. Your very self is meant to be a temple where God's Spirit dwells, and where prayer, communion with God, is central. But what happens to us sinners? The moneychangers and the merchants enter in. What is supposed to be a place of prayer becomes a den of thieves.

And so, the Lord must do in us now what he did in the temple then: a little house-cleaning. What shape is the temple of your soul in? Suppose that Jesus has made a whip of cords, knotted with the Ten Commandments. What would he clear out of you? What, through the prayer of contrition, is it time to crush within you?

Adoration and Right Praise

"ADORATION" is derived from *adoratio* (*ad ora*; literally, "to the mouth"). To pray in a stance of adoration is to be mouth to mouth with God, breathing in his divine life and breathing out praise. The opening line of the Song of Solomon—"Let him kiss me with the kisses of his mouth!" (Song of Sol. 1:2)—can be seen not only as a cry of erotic desire but also as a longing of the soul for worship. Mouth to mouth, one is also "reconciled" to God—literally eyelash to eyelash with him (from the Latin *cilia*). So aligned, everything in the worshiper becomes properly ordered.

In the attitude of adoration, Adam, the first man, was accordingly the first priest, and the ordered garden that surrounded him can be construed as the primordial temple. Right praise (*ortho doxa*) leads to the right ordering of the person who gives praise, and it also conduces toward the right ordering of the family, community, society, and cosmos that surround that person. In this context, we can understand a remark often associated with Dorothy Day and Peter Maurin, the founders of the Catholic Worker Movement: "Cult cultivates the culture." Business, finance, politics, sports, the arts, entertainment, and so on—all these find their proper place and realize their proper finality when they are grounded in the praise of God. One could read the liturgical prayer "Glory to God in the highest, and on earth peace to people of good will" not only as a word of praise but also as a kind of formula: when glory is given to God above all things, then peace breaks out among us.

Original sin can be appreciated as the suspension of right praise, the consequence of a failure in priesthood. When Adam and Eve listened to the voice of the serpent and disobeyed the command of God, they fell out of the stance of adoration and ordered their hearts away from the unconditioned good. This led to interior disintegration: the falling apart of mind from flesh, soul from body, intention from action, and so on. It also gave rise to the disintegration of community and alienation from nature. The expulsion of Adam and Eve from the garden should not be interpreted as a sentence passed by an insulted deity, but rather as the inevitable consequence of bad praise. When something other than God is given glory in the highest, the garden turns into a desert. Therefore, the entirety of the biblical narrative could be read as the story of God's attempts to lure his people back into right praise, not because God needs such devotion, but precisely because such devotion is tantamount to human flourishing.

When sin resulted in the destruction of the entirety of the created order, God sent a rescue operation in the form of a great ship on which a microcosm of Eden was preserved. This is why Noah can be read as a priestly figure presiding over a tiny remnant where right praise was practiced. Once the floodwaters receded, Noah the priest offered a sacrifice to God and allowed the good order that he had preserved to flood the world, reconstituting it as a temple.

As God shaped his people Israel, he consistently coupled covenant with sacrificial worship. Thus Abram, having heard the promise that his descendants would be more numerous than the stars, was asked to sacrifice five animals to God, cutting their bodies in two (Gen. 15:5–11). Moses received the word of God on Mount Sinai and then slaughtered bulls and sprinkled their blood on the altar and on the people (Exod. 24:1–8). In Exodus, Leviticus, and Deuteronomy, we read detailed prescriptions governing the offering of sacrifice to God, oblations that took place in a tabernacle or tent sanctuary that accompanied the wandering people in the desert.

Why was the worship that God demanded sacrificial in form? Prior to the fall, adoration was effortless; but after the tumble into sin, right praise came only at a cost. This is because heterodoxy ("false praise") twisted the human person out of shape, setting mind against will, body against spirit, passion against passion, and so on. The recovery of one's spiritual equilibrium, therefore, was necessarily painful. The action of bringing an animal to the tabernacle (and later to the temple) for sacrifice was an implicit statement that what was happening to that animal should by rights be happening to the offerer of sacrifice.

This history of sacrifice reaches its culmination on the cross, where Jesus, the perfect priest and the New Adam, gives right praise to the Father, even while bearing the sins of the world. And the prayer of the Mass, the

Eucharistic liturgy, is a re-presentation of the sacrifice of Jesus, bringing the power of the cross to bear in the present. It is, therefore, the place of right praise *par excellence*.

Give Thanks in All Circumstances

ST. PAUL'S FIRST LETTER TO THE THESSALONIANS dates probably from around the year 50, and has the distinction of being one of the earliest Christian texts we possess. Toward the end of his letter, Paul is summing up his message to the little community that he had founded. We ought to pay very close attention, for this represents the effort of the first great evangelist to sum up the Christian way of life, and it culminates in an emphasis on the prayer of thanksgiving.

He says, "Rejoice always, pray without ceasing, give thanks in all circumstances; for this is the will of God in Christ Jesus for you" (1 Thess. 5:16–18). Paul is not exactly known for his measured and moderate statements, but these are extraordinary, even for him. We would understand it well enough if he said "Cheer up, things aren't so bad" or "Increase the time you spend in prayer" or "Remember to give thanks from time to time for all of God's benefits." But no: "Always . . . without ceasing . . . in all circumstances."

Isn't this just a bit over the top? Sure, we should rejoice, but "always"? When we are bored, depressed, or anxious? When a beloved friend is sick, when a family member dies, when we receive a terrible diagnosis? It seems bizarre even to suggest. Likewise, we should pray, but "without ceasing"? How could we possibly do this, even if we all became, tomorrow, Trappist monks and nuns? Even they don't pray without ceasing. Does this leave no room for the entertainment, play, and work of ordinary life? Keeping a daily Holy Hour can be hard enough—but a holy *twenty-four* hours, every day? Finally, we should certainly give thanks, but "in all circumstances"? We should thank God for the worst things in life—for sickness, failure, loss of money, personal insults?

As you might suspect, this passage from 1 Thessalonians has intrigued and beguiled some of the finest theological minds in the great tradition, and their exploration of it is of tremendous importance. Here is the principle that is key to understanding what Paul means: God is not one competitive being among many, but rather, as Thomas Aquinas put it, the sheer act of being itself. This means, practically, that God grounds, undergirds, and involves himself in all aspects of reality. He doesn't simply "intervene" from time to time; he is steadily present to all things. Relatedly, as Jean-Pierre de Caussade put it, everything that happens to us is, directly or indirectly, an expression of the will of God. Whatever exists has been either directly willed by God or permitted by God as part of his providential design.

Now, with this in mind, go back to Paul's recommendations. What would it mean to "pray without ceasing"? It would mean to see God active in all things. To pray means to turn one's face to God, to look steadily at God. Once this becomes a habit, we see God in and through all things. We don't so much single him out as one thing among many, but rather see him as the ground of all existence.

Once we learn how to pray always, then we can indeed rejoice always. There are, obviously, some things, people, and experiences that make us, in the immediate sense, more joyful than others. And we *should* enjoy them. But once we understand that God's will stands behind absolutely everything that we experience, then we can find that deep joy that the Bible calls "peace" all the time. It's not that we ignore bad things or move into a la-la land of self-deception; real Christians look evil and disappointment in the face. But they see behind it something else. This explains the extraordinary insouciance of the saints, the peace that they experience despite any trial.

And once we learn how to pray in all circumstances, then we can indeed give thanks in all circumstances. Everything that exists holds its being as a gift. In light of this sheer gratuitousness of creation, the only proper response—both to the beauty and goodness we experience and the suffering and hardship we endure—is one of gratitude and admiration. Moreover, everything that happens to us is, directly or indirectly, an expression of God's will and therefore something for which we should give thanks.

Many years ago, I went on an eight-day Jesuit retreat. The first night, I had a session with my spiritual father, and he told me to recall all of the best experiences of my life and give thanks for them. When I returned the next day, I recounted to him the fruit of my prayer. He smiled benignly and then said, "Now I want you to spend a couple of hours in prayer, remembering all of the worst moments of your life—all of your suffering, failure, embarrassment—and then I want you to thank God for those!" He intuited that I had benefitted perhaps even more from the negative experiences than the positive ones.

Rejoice always, pray without ceasing, give thanks in all circumstances!

12

Prayer of Petition

I IMAGINE THAT when most people hear the word "prayer," they probably think of asking God for something. And, indeed, petitionary prayer is one of the most fundamental ways that we raise our minds and hearts to God. It is also the commonest form of prayer in the Bible. Every major scriptural character—Abraham, Isaac, Jacob, Joseph, Moses, Joshua, Samuel, David, Solomon, Ezra, Nehemiah, Peter, James, Paul, and John—prays in this way; they all ask God for things. There is something, of course, primal and elemental about this kind of prayer: "O God, please help me!" "O Lord, save my child!" If we could place a net capable of catching prayers as they waft their way to heaven from hospitals and churches, we would corral millions upon millions of them. Finally, the paradigmatic prayer that Jesus taught us—the Our Father—is nothing but a series of petitions, and Jesus urged his followers, again and again, to persevere in prayer: "Ask, and it will be given you; search, and you will find; knock, and the door will be opened for you" (Matt. 7:7).

Even though this form of prayer seems simpler and more basic than others, in fact, it is more difficult to make sense of theologically. When we speak of petitionary prayer, dilemmas and anomalies emerge that have puzzled religious thinkers for centuries. If God cannot change, what is the point of asking him for anything? And if God is omniscient, what is the point of telling him what you need? Keep in mind that the same Jesus who told us to ask and ask again also informed us that God "knows what you need before you ask him" (Matt. 6:8).

One way to shed light on this problem is to refer to the biblical master metaphor for God—namely, the parent. Throughout the Bible, God is referred to as a father and even in some texts as a mother: "Can a woman forget her nursing child?" (Isa. 49:15); "Nurse and be satisfied from her consoling breast" (Isa. 66:11). Parents hear petitions from their children constantly, persistent requests for things, some good and some quite bad—and decent parents know what their child needs long before she asks for it. But none of this conduces a parent toward stifling those requests or pronouncing them useless—even if he is obliged frequently to respond negatively. God indeed knows everything about everything, so he is aware of what we need before we ask; yet still, like a good parent, he delights in hearing our requests—and like a good parent, he does not always respond the way we would like him to.

St. Augustine offers another perspective on our dilemma. God wants us to ask, seek, and petition persistently not in order that he might be changed but that *we* might be changed. Through the initial refusal to give us what we want, God compels our hearts to expand in order to receive adequately what he wants to give us. In the very process of hungering and thirsting for certain goods, we make ourselves worthy vessels. It is not as though in petitioning God we are approaching a stubborn pasha or big city boss whom we hope might be persuaded by our persistence. Rather, it is God who works a sort of spiritual alchemy in us by forcing us to wait. In his treatment of the Lord's Prayer, Thomas Aquinas tells us, very much in the spirit of Augustine, that the initial petition of the Our Father, "hallowed be thy name," is not asking for something to change in God, for God's name is always holy; it is asking that God might work a change in us so that we hallow God above all things.

Aquinas provides what I take to be the richest theological framework for petitionary prayer when he speaks of God praying through us. Aquinas is convinced that God, as the unmoved mover, can never be changed by our prayer; nevertheless, God can arrange his providential governance of the universe in such a way that what he wants to give will be coordinated with our asking for it. On this reading, whatever is good and right and true in our prayer is God already praying in us, adjusting our desire to his desire. Since God is noncompetitive with his creation—since he is not the supreme being but the very ground of being—his "invasion" enhances us, makes us more authentically free. A very good example of this dynamic is a liturgical prayer from the feast of Augustine's mother, St. Monica. The text begins as follows: "O God, who console the sorrowful and who mercifully accepted the motherly tears of Saint Monica for the conversion of her son Augustine . . ." Mind you, it does not say that the tears of Monica moved God to act or compelled him somehow to change the structure of his providence; it says that God accepted those tears in coordination with granting the grace of conversion to her son, implying that God himself was effectively crying through the tears of Monica.

Part IV

Contemplative Prayer

13

John of the Cross and the Dark Night of the Soul

IN HIS POEM "The Living Flame of Love," St. John of the Cross—a great mystic, reformer of the Carmelites, and Doctor of the Church—offers a powerful image of the human soul. We human beings, he says, have within us "great caverns," which are infinitely deep, unfathomable. These are intellect, will, and feeling—and they are infinite, precisely because they are ordered to God. The mind eagerly comes to know particular things, individual truths, but none of these achievements finally settles the mind; just the contrary. The will reaches out to particular goods, but no limited good ever fully satisfies it. Finally, our souls order us to beauty and justice. But no matter how much beauty we take in, we always want more; in fact, the greater the beauty, the greater our appetite for beauty is whetted.

This spiritual anthropology helps to explain why most of us are so unhappy most of the time. I don't mean that most of us are psychologically depressed; I mean that our infinite desire never meets in the world an object commensurate with it. And thus, even as we experience great joy, we still twist and reach with a restless dissatisfaction, like the figures on Michelangelo's Sistine Chapel ceiling. John of the Cross uses his image of the infinitely deep caverns to diagnose the fundamental spiritual disorder that we all share—namely, trying to fill those caverns with the petty goods of the finite world: pleasure, sex, power, and prestige. This drive leads, inexorably, to addiction and hence to deeper dissatisfaction. Or maybe we cover the caverns over, pretending that they don't exist. This is the characteristic pathology of contemporary materialism and secularism: convincing ourselves, even as we are starving spiritually, that we're perfectly full.

The good news, as far as John of the Cross is concerned, is that this subterfuge, this illusion created by the ego, cannot possibly endure, and the person must finally awaken to the insufficiency of the world. That is when he turns, perhaps in desperation, to the infinite. That is when he seeks, almost despite himself, to raise his mind and heart to God.

John of the Cross' dark night is often used as a metaphor for depression or loss of direction, but that is not at all how John meant it. If the soul is to order itself to God, it must rid itself of attachments to anything creaturely. That is, it must overcome its tendency to turn something less than God into God, and it must accordingly purge and let go of idols. It is most important to note that this purging hasn't a thing to do with a puritanical disdain for the body or the cultivation of a *fuga mundi* (flight from the world) spirituality. John of the Cross fully shares the biblical and Catholic sense of the goodness of creation. The process of the dark night has to do with the proper ordering of desire: God first, everything else second and for the sake of God.

The purgative process unfolds in two steps, what John calls "the dark night of the senses" and "the dark night of the soul." During the first phase, a person detaches himself from every sensual good or pleasure that has taken central position in his life. He lets go of food, drink, sex, and sensible delight in the measure that these have become soul-ordering values. In terms of the life of Jesus, the dark night of the senses would correspond to the Lord's long fast in the desert and his resistance to the tempter's suggestion that he turn stones into bread.

Once the dark night of the senses is complete, one is ready to enter into the purgative discipline of the dark night of the soul. During this process, the seeker learns to detach himself from those more rarified substitutes for God, which are the concepts, ideas, and images of the mind. There are spiritually alert people who have managed to free themselves from the more ordinary distractions but who are nevertheless beguiled by the products of their own religious consciousness, which are every bit as creaturely as food and drink and fame. These, too, have to be set aside, let go of. At this point, we can see why the image of the dark night has come to be associated with depression, for this purgative path is indeed painful, sometimes wrenchingly so. If one's life has been ordered around the love of some creaturely value, then the reordering process will cost dearly. There is, accordingly, indeed something austere about John's spiritual style. A story has been told about a younger Carmelite colleague of his who was a deeply spiritual man. One day, he told John how much he loved a particular crucifix that had been given to him and that had proven a wonderful aid to prayer. John bluntly told him to surrender it, for it had become an object of attachment. Once again, this is neither cruelty nor fussy puritanism; it is honesty and clarity in regard to the demands of the dark night.

I confess that I hesitated to share that anecdote because I am loath to leave the impression that John of the Cross was nothing but a dyspeptic ascetic. He saw the dark night in both of its stages as merely preparatory, a conduit to a blissful experience of God. When the purgations are complete, the soul is ready for the journey into God, or, better, it is ready to receive the gift that God wants to give. Consider these gorgeous lines from John's poem on the dark night, composed during his awful sojourn in what amounted to a prison cell in Toledo after being seized by his Carmelite brothers:

> One dark night,
> fired with love's urgent longings
> —ah, the sheer grace!—
> I went out unseen,
> my house being now all stilled.

The stilled house symbolizes the soul that has passed through the dark night and has found rest from its addictive patterns of desire. But notice that the stillness is not an end in itself. Once the errant desires have been quieted, that deep, abiding, infinite desire can surface; "love's urgent longings" can at last be felt. And then the soul is ready for its journey toward God:

> On that glad night,
> in secret, for no one saw me,
> nor did I look at anything,
> with no other light or guide
> than the one that burned in my heart.

Since it represents liberation, the night is "glad"; and since the soul has rid itself of any need for approval or fame, it exults in the fact that no one sees it; and since it no longer relies on worldly goods, it doesn't "look at anything"; and, finally, since the deepest desire of the heart has surfaced, the soul knows precisely where to go, needing "no other guide" than that very longing. This last idea finds an echo in "The Living Flame of Love," where John speaks of those infinite caverns being illumined by the light and heat of God.

Then come these lines, evocative of the high point of mystical union with God:

> Upon my flowering breast
> which I kept wholly for him alone,
> there he lay sleeping,
> and I caressing him. . . .
>
> I abandoned and forgot myself,
> laying my face on my Beloved;
> all things ceased; I went out from myself,
> leaving my cares
> forgotten among the lilies.

Is there anywhere in the literature of the world a more compelling and beautiful description of union with

God? In order to indicate what it is like to be, at last, in possession of the God who alone can satisfy the deepest aching of the heart, John reaches, naturally enough, for erotic language, the imagery of sexual intimacy. His heart (the "breast" in the imagery of the poem) has all along been ordered to God, though through much of his life he had allowed this truth to become obscured. Now, having gone through the dark night, he is ready to receive the one he was always destined to receive: "there he lay sleeping, / and I caressing him." Finally, he imagines himself face to face with God, literally in the attitude of *adoratio*. At the climax of the spiritual journey is the recovery of Eden, the restoration of the easy friendship that Adam enjoyed with God, the realization of the worship foreshadowed in the temple.

14

Teresa of Avila and Finding the Center

PERHAPS THE MOST IMPORTANT FIGURE in the life of John of the Cross was Teresa of Avila, the Carmelite nun who inaugurated the reform movement in which John participated. As Teresa entered her forties, she began to receive a series of mystical visitations. She would see Christ, the Blessed Mother, and the saints, not so much with her bodily eyes as with the eyes of her mind and imagination. It would be wrong to dismiss these experiences as mere subjective fantasies, for they came to her unannounced and struck her with overwhelming and often disconcerting power. During these intense encounters, she would typically pass into an ecstatic trance, sometimes lying motionless for up to half an hour. Other times, she was known to levitate. There are even stories told of some of the stronger nuns being called upon to pull her back to the ground when she would take off! The most famous of these mystical encounters was what came to be called the "transverberation," which Teresa vividly describes in her autobiography. It was this scene of an angel piercing

Teresa's heart that Gian Lorenzo Bernini so unforgetta-
bly immortalized in marble, vividly calling to mind John
of the Cross' erotic analogies.

What can we moderns, we inheritors of the skeptical
scientific turn, make of all this? To be sure, such experiences are, even within the religious tradition, rare, and
Teresa would be the first to insist that they don't constitute the heart of the matter, spiritually speaking. Her
disciple John of the Cross, in fact, said that extraordinary
visions should be taken in and then promptly let go of.
Nevertheless, they do seem to play a role—from biblical
times to the present day—in the divine economy. Might
God not deign, occasionally, to signal his presence in a
remarkable and vivid way? Might he not, at privileged
times, allow the supernatural world to manifest itself in
this ordinary world? Might he not, as Flannery O'Connor
put it, shout "to the hard of hearing" in order to remind
us of his existence? In a word, we can make too much of
Teresa's encounters, but at the same time, we can make
too little of them.

At the prompting of her spiritual directors, Teresa began to write down her experiences in prayer for
the benefit of her Carmelite sisters, and the books she
composed—*The Interior Castle*, *The Book of Her Life*, and
The Way of Perfection, among others—constitute some of
the gems of the Catholic spiritual tradition. What stands
at the heart of her teaching? To understand what she was
trying essentially to communicate, it is best to look at the
title of her most famous work. Teresa of Avila discovered,
at the very depth of her soul, Christ dwelling in her, and
this divine presence, she said, was like an interior castle.

Consider what this image would have conveyed

to a sixteenth-century Spaniard. A castle was a keep, a place of safety and power, shelter from the storm. To be grounded in Christ, Teresa realized, was to be rooted in the very power that is here and now creating the cosmos, in the God who is beyond the vagaries of space and time. Most of us sinners seek to anchor our lives in some worldly good, but these earthly attachments are necessarily evanescent and therefore unsatisfying. They are vulnerable to corruption, criticism, wear and tear, the shifting moods of the crowd, and final dissolution. None of them—pleasure, money, power, honor—is, in a word, a castle. But Christ is—and that is why the wise person reorients his life toward him, seeks refuge in him, leans on him. Teresa essentially echoes Paul's "It is no longer I who live, but it is Christ who lives in me" (Gal. 2:20). The ego, with all of its preoccupations and false moves, all of its contradictory desires and flimsy defenses, is unreliable; but the inner Christ—eternal, omnipotent, commanding, clear—is like a rock, a redoubt, a castle.

In so many of the spiritual masters we find the theme of the center—which is to say, the divine still point around which the entirety of the self properly revolves. Worship involves turning the entire self toward God. Meister Eckhart, a fourteenth-century Dominican spiritual writer, speaks of the *Seelengrund* (the ground of the soul) as the point where God and the creature meet in friendship, and John of the Cross described the "inner wine cellar," the place where, at the depth of the soul, the "spirits" are kept, a place of intoxication and elevation. Ignatius of Loyola, the founder of the Jesuit order and a contemporary of both Teresa and John, made detachment, or what he called "indifference," the organizing principle of his spirituality. He famously wrote, "We must make ourselves indifferent to all created things. . . . We should not prefer health to sickness, riches to poverty, honor to dishonor, a long life to a short life." That kind of insouciance can come only from having made contact with the center. Teresa's interior castle is still another evocation of this "place" where the soul rests confidently in Christ and where a mystical marriage unfolds.

In light of these considerations, we recall Teresa's most famous prayer, one that can only be uttered from the center:

> Let nothing disturb you;
> Let nothing frighten you.
> All things are passing.
> God never changes.
> Patience obtains all things.
> Nothing is wanting to him who possesses God.
> God alone suffices.

All of this takes on a new resonance when one visits Teresa's hometown and sees the miles of castellated walls that surround and protect it. Teresa came of age as a nun and mystic within the confines of a great castle, and she came to realize that those exterior walls were but a fleeting and creaturely sign of the ramparts and castle within.

15

Thomas Merton and the Virginal Point

SPEAKING OF PRAYER usually puts us in mind of rather alien figures: medieval monks in their choir stalls or perhaps hermits squirreled away in their desert huts. I believe that hermits and monks have a great deal to teach us, but there is someone much closer to our own time and temperament, someone who tramped through Times Square and frequented the jazz clubs of Manhattan in the first half of the twentieth century, a spiritual teacher who emerged from the maelstrom of contemporary doubt and secularism.

When Thomas Merton's autobiography, *The Seven Storey Mountain*, which chronicles his conversion, was published in 1948, it caused a sensation and contributed mightily to a spiritual revival across the United States and to an awakening of interest in the ancient traditions of mysticism of which most Americans were simply unaware. This very contemporary figure remains, therefore, a privileged portal through which twenty-first-century seekers can explore the meaning of prayer. What motivated someone who experienced so many of the anxieties and opportunities of our time finally to dedicate his life to raising his mind and heart to God?

The pivotal theme of Merton's writings, throughout the 1940s, '50s, and '60s, was contemplation, the form of prayer that he learned from John of the Cross. Merton insisted, over and over again, that contemplation ought not to be seen as an arcane practice of certain spiritual athletes but as something that stands at the heart of the Christian thing, since it is nothing other than the organization of a person's life around the divine center. In language redolent of Teresa, John of the Cross, and Meister Eckhart, Merton spoke of *le point vierge* (the virginal point), which is the place of contact between the soul and Christ. He characterized contemplative prayer as finding that place in you where you are here and now being created by God. That magnificent description was born of Merton's discovery, many years before, of Étienne Gilson's notion of the divine aseity. If God is that which exists through the power of his own essence, then whatever else exists must come forth in its totality from the creative power of God. Creation, then, is not only an event "at the beginning of time"; it is something happening right now. To pray contemplatively is to find the place at the very bottom of one's being—the *point vierge*, the interior castle, the inner wine cellar—where God's life and love are sustaining you in existence. Once that center is found, everything else changes. When we find that place, we necessarily find that which connects us to everyone else and everything else in the cosmos.

This helps to explain why Merton wrote so energetically about nonviolence in the 1960s. Some see this as a surrender to trendiness on Merton's part and an abandonment of the more classically Catholic spirituality he espoused earlier in his life, but I believe that this is a superficial reading. In speaking incisively against atomic weapons and against the war in Vietnam, Merton was drawing practical moral conclusions from creation metaphysics and from the contemplative prayer that gave him access to the divine center. Merton consistently denied that he was a strict pacifist in the manner of Francis of Assisi or Dorothy Day; he insisted that practitioners of the Catholic spiritual tradition, adepts of contemplation, should always exercise a fundamental option for nonviolence, for their prayer must teach them that all people, despite whatever political or cultural conflicts might divide them, always remain, at the deepest level, siblings.

On March 18, 1958, Merton was in Louisville for some practical business and found himself at the corner of Fourth and Walnut Streets in the heart of the shopping district. In that ordinary place, he had an experience in some ways as extraordinary as Teresa of Avila's encounter with the angel: "I was suddenly overwhelmed with the realization that I loved all those people, that they were mine and I theirs, that we could not be alien to one another even though we were total strangers. It was like waking from a dream of separateness."

Merton had come to the Trappist Abbey of Our Lady of Gethsemani to escape the world, in the negative sense of that term, and to do penance for his sins. In the course of his long retreat (at the time of the Louisville experience, he had been seventeen years in the monastery), he had moved, through contemplative prayer, deep into the center. And it was from that place that this mystical perception of union was born. "This sense of liberation from an illusory difference was such a relief and such a joy to me that I almost laughed out loud. And I suppose my happiness could have taken form in the words, 'Thank God, thank God that I am like other men.'" Merton clearly sees the paradox that it was precisely his contemplative isolation that made this experience possible: "This changes nothing in the sense and value of my solitude, for it is in fact the function of solitude to make one realize such things." He also sees the Christological dimension of this moment: "I have the immense joy of being *man*, a member of a race in which God Himself became incarnate." We are linked to one another not only through our common creation but also by the universality of the Mystical Body of Jesus. Here is how Merton summed up this ecstatic experience: "And if only everybody could realize this! But it cannot be explained. There is no way of telling people that they are all walking around shining like the sun."

Somehow, in that humdrum place in downtown Louisville, it all came together for Merton: metaphysics, creation, Incarnation, contemplation, nonviolence, and universal love. And this grandeur of vision, this unification of thought and action, this sense of getting what it is all about is the effect of real prayer, of raising the mind and heart to God.

Part V

Liturgical Prayer

Part 9

The Mass

THE MASS—the most important practice of prayer—is "the source and summit of the Christian life." It is the action that most fully displays who we Christians distinctively are. When Thomas Merton was ordained a priest, he invited a number of his friends, many of them non-Catholic, to attend his first Mass. One of them, Seymour Freedgood, a Jew, asked the new priest, "What exactly is the Mass?" Expecting a more or less pietistic answer, Freedgood was surprised when Merton responded, "It is a kind of ballet, with similar prescribed movements and gestures." I have always savored Merton's answer because it captures the iconic/artistic dimension of the liturgy; in its gathering, singing, signing, reading, listening, praying, offering, processing, communicating, sending, and being sent, the Body of Christ iconically acts out who it is—to the glory of God and for the transformation of the world.

In the book of Revelation, the visionary John is offered a glimpse of heaven. He sees a throne room, where a King sits in splendor, surrounded by a group of robed elders who perform acts of worship and obeisance. He also spies an altar, candlesticks, and myriads of saints waving palm branches; the Lamb of God "standing as if it had been slaughtered" (Rev. 5:6) who opens a sacred text; and an angel who swings a large censer. It is hard to avoid the conclusion that we are dealing here with what the council fathers at Vatican II called the "heavenly liturgy," the ballet of praise that takes place in God's eternal household. What the mainstream of the Christian tradition has preserved is the conviction that when we gather for praise of God, we are doing much more than merely seeking inspiration or fellowship. We are in fact consciously aligning ourselves to the celestial dance, hoping that some of its peacefulness, beauty, and order might become ours, that God's will be done "on earth as it is in heaven." We are imitating the great practice that is eternal life.

Let us look at several dimensions of the liturgical act. The book of Revelation tells us that around God's throne is "a great multitude that no one could count, from every nation, from all tribes and peoples and languages" (Rev. 7:9). When Dorothy Day was experiencing a religious awakening and began to attend Mass on a regular basis, she was especially struck by the egalitarian and inclusive way that people gathered for the liturgy. The usual social distinctions, she noticed, were blurred, as rich and poor, educated and ignorant, members of establishment families and immigrants all came together in the same place for the same purpose. The assembled community, the Body of Christ, in which there is "no longer Jew or Greek, there is no longer slave or free, there is no longer male or female" (Gal. 3:28), is itself a countercultural sign, a challenge to an antagonistic social ontology.

The prayer itself formally begins with the sign of the cross, the invocation of the Trinitarian persons. We remember that the Christian prays not so much *to* God as *inside* of God, from within the love of Father, Son, and Holy Spirit. And so the liturgical ballet commences with an evocation of this divine *communio* (the Father forgetting himself in love for the Son, the Son emptying himself in love for the Father, the Spirit the mutual breathing forth of the love of Father and Son) and the hope that we might learn to move in accord with its rhythms. In the symbol of Christ's cross, we nestle within the space opened up by the Trinitarian persons and thus find our deepest center.

Next, the community sings *Kyrie, eleison; Christe, eleison; Kyrie, eleison* (Lord, have mercy; Christ, have mercy; Lord, have mercy)—three times admitting sinfulness, and three times asking for the divine transformation. Christians in liturgical prayer are compelled to acknowledge that their *communio* is incomplete, that it is an inadequate icon of God's *communio.* But we remember that it is only the centered saint who can say, "Lord, have mercy."

Next, the Scriptures are read. Christians stand firmly in the Pauline tradition that *fides ex auditu* (faith comes from what is heard; Rom. 10:17). The assumptions of subjectivizing modernity notwithstanding, they know that faith does not well up from common human experience or from the structures of the psyche, but rather comes from without as a revelation, literally an unveiling, of a truth that would be otherwise unavailable. Christians discover who God is, what constitutes the sacred world, who they are and ought to be, precisely by listening to the oddly textured narratives of the Bible. They learn to be holy by attending to the cast of characters—saints, rogues, prophets, sinners—on display in the biblical stories, and especially by watching the great Character who acts, sometimes directly, sometimes indirectly, in every story.

The homily or sermon effects a correlation between this biblical narrative and the experience of the community. Mind you, it is not a correlation in the sense of bringing together secular questions and sacred answers; rather, it is a drawing up of the lived world into the biblical patterns, or a laying of the latter on the former as a kind of interpretive grid. As they listen to the Word in the liturgical assembly, Christians realize that they don't tell their own story—as the modern mythology of freedom would have it—but rather that they already belong to a Story and that their freedom is authentically discovered in relation to that narrative.

After hearing the Word of God, worshiping Christians perform one of the spiritual works of mercy: they pray for one another, especially for the sick, the needy, and the dead. Rooted together in the divine center, Christians know that they are connected to one another and that they, accordingly, must bear each other's burdens in love. They pray for each other because there is no cell or organ in the Body of Christ that functions in isolation. The recitation of prayers on behalf of the weak also serves a very practical function: it lets the community know who is suffering and thus focuses their own exercise of the corporal and spiritual works of mercy.

Signed by the Trinitarian love, aware of their sins, formed by the Word, strengthened as a body, the community is now ready for the properly Eucharistic (literally, "thanksgiving") phase of the liturgy. We give thanks to God the Father for the gift of his Son by presenting the most precious offering we have: that very gift. After joining our voices, in the great "Holy, holy, holy," to those of the angels (the heavenly *communio*), we turn our attention to the elements of bread and wine. The priest, acting in the very person of Christ, pronounces the words that Jesus said the night before he died: "Take this, all of you, and eat of it, for this is my Body, which will be given up for you"; "Take this, all of you, and drink from it, for this is the chalice of my Blood." In this inexhaustibly mysterious act, Jesus identifies himself with the elements in such a way that they become the bearers of his very presence. Jesus, crucified and risen, stands in our midst, as he did with the two disciples on the road to Emmaus, as he did with the Eleven in the upper room, as he did with Peter and John on the shore of the Sea of Tiberias. The center opens, and we enter in. United with the Son, we become, in him, a sacrifice pleasing to the Father.

The priest then holds up the Host and the chalice and says, "Behold the Lamb of God, behold him who takes away the sins of the world. Blessed are those called to the supper of the Lamb." We are meant not simply to admire the Lamb of God but to consume him, making him bone of our bone and flesh of our flesh. Jesus said, "I am the vine, you are the branches" (John 15:5), and, "Unless you eat the flesh of the Son of Man and drink his blood, you have no life in you" (John 6:53), indicating that our relationship to him is organic. Finally, at the climax of the liturgy, we commune with Christ and, in Christ, with one another, solidifying our corporate identity. The social ontology of forgiveness, thanksgiving, and mutual care becomes, in that moment, densely real, not just a hope but an accomplished fact.

At the close of the liturgy, the priest pronounces the simple words "Go forth, the Mass is ended." It has been said that these are, after the words of consecration themselves, the most sacred words of the liturgy. Having visited the center and been formed as the Body of Christ, the worshipers are sent out in order to sanctify the world, drawing it into the pattern of what has been realized at the Mass: "Thy kingdom come, thy will be done, on earth as it is in heaven." The *communio* of love that is heaven has been reflected iconically in the *communio* of the Eucharistic assembly—and now that icon is meant to be an exemplar to the fallen and dysfunctional world. There is nothing inward-looking or sectarian about the liturgy. As commentators as diverse as Jacques Maritain, Reynold Hillenbrand, Virgil Michel, and Dorothy Day saw, the connection between the Eucharist and social justice is an essential one, since each is the mirror image of the other. A basic conviction of the Christian Church is that proper praise of God produces in us a likeness unto God. And thus the liturgy is the practice that fosters a conformity to the Practice that is the Trinity.

And so, in iconically displaying the divine life in the liturgy, Christians know that their lives are not about them; they are related to the infinite mystery of God and always about his missionary purposes.

17

The Liturgy of the Hours

"SEVEN TIMES A DAY I PRAISE YOU" (Ps. 119:164). This line from the longest of the Psalms is the inspiration behind the monastic tradition of giving praise to God over the course of seven designated times or "hours" every day: Matins or Vigil (prayer in the middle of the night); Lauds (morning prayer); Terce ("third" hour of the day); Sext ("sixth" hour of the day); None ("ninth" hour of the day); Vespers (evening prayer); and Compline (night prayer). A somewhat encapsulated version of this tradition is contained in the Liturgy of the Hours or "Divine Office"— the official prayer of the Church by which, in a structured way, the hours of the day are sanctified.

Every priest is obligated to pray the Liturgy of the Hours, making the formal promise at their diaconate ordination. In fact, while a priest is not obligated to say Mass every day—though most priests do in the course of their pastoral work—he *is* obliged to pray the Office every day. So it is, in a way, a more sacred obligation. An older priest I knew once recalled a story to me: He was coming back from an event late at night and realized he had not read his Office. So, he pulled the car over to the side of the road and, by the light of the headlights, began praying. Another driver, thinking that the priest must be in some kind of trouble, pulled over and offered to help. "Oh no," the priest responded. "I am just reading my book." To which the man responded: "That must be a heck of a good book!" That priest was serious about his obligation.

But while priests are obligated to pray the Liturgy of the Hours, I would also happily recommend this practice to any Catholic. Like daily Mass, it is a great prayer of the Church, and any baptized person is invited to participate in it. The mission of the laity is, as the Second Vatican Council taught, to go out and sanctify the world, not to enter into a monastic frame of mind. Nevertheless, that mission must be *informed* by prayer, and that can include praying the Liturgy of the Hours—not necessarily the whole Office, but perhaps simply Morning Prayer and Evening Prayer, the Office of Readings, or Night Prayer at the end of the day. Whatever portion works or that you find yourself drawn to, let its rhythm inform your spiritual life as you work to sanctify the secular order.

Why is the Liturgy of the Hours such an important pillar of the Church's prayer—indeed, the Church's highest form of prayer after the Mass? First, because it is intensely biblical. The Liturgy of the Hours does include various passages from the Church Fathers and conciliar documents, but it is made up primarily of Scripture. This includes the Our Father (Matt. 6:9–13) and three Lucan canticles focused on the Incarnation: the Benedictus (the Canticle of Zachariah—Luke 1:68–79) in Morning Prayer, the Magnificat (the Canticle of Mary—Luke 1:46–55) in Evening Prayer, and the Nunc Dimittis (the Canticle of

Simeon—Luke 2:29–32) in Night Prayer. But the heart of the Liturgy of the Hours is the Psalms. These prayers link you, in a powerful way, to the great tradition of the Church: Thomas Aquinas, Augustine, and Jesus himself knew and prayed these same Psalms.

But the Liturgy of the Hours is not only the prayer *of* the Church; it is also, consciously and intentionally, the prayer *for* the Church. We always pray in and for the Mystical Body. Whenever my seminary students would complain that they weren't always in the mood to pray the Hours, I would respond, "So what? You're not saying this prayer for yourself and your own edification primarily; you are praying on behalf of the Church." You are praying for those who can't, or won't, pray for themselves. During Night Prayer on Friday, we always pray Psalm 88, a prayer of great desperation: "I have reached the end of my strength, like one alone among the dead; like the slain lying in their graves. . . . My one companion is darkness." Even if you aren't personally feeling what the Psalmist is feeling, trust me: someone in the Body of Christ is. You are praying on behalf of that person and in union with that person. The same goes for Psalms of joy: even if you're not in the mood that day to jump up and down, somebody else in the Body of Christ is, and you are exalting for them.

Praying the Hours can be demanding; the sheer amount of time involved in working through the prayers and other texts every day is an obstacle for many people. For priests engaged in a busy pastoral life and laypeople navigating the obligations of work and family, it can be a struggle to enter into its rhythm, especially at first. For those using the full books instead of audio and apps, there is also the complexity of navigating the texts, which typically involves several placeholding ribbons and frequent flipping back and forth to find the appropriate readings. But as with learning an instrument or playing a sport, dedication is key. In good times and in bad, when you're into it and when you're not, stay with it. As Aristotle saw, we become habituated to virtue over time, bringing our feelings on line with our actions. So it goes with praying the Liturgy of the Hours: over time, it will simply become a part of your life, and your appreciation for its riches will deepen.

18

The Creed

A PECULIAR QUALITY OF CHRISTIANITY is that, among all
the major religions of the world, it is most concerned
with doctrinal clarity. Unlike a number of faiths that
emphasize orthopraxis (right behavior) more than orthodoxy (right belief) and unlike others that cultivate a
more open-ended and less defined theology, Christianity has, from the beginning, been massively interested in
laying out its beliefs clearly, succinctly, and articulately.
This instinct has found expression in creeds—which is
to say, formal statements of doctrinal belief. Of the many
such documents that emerged in the first centuries of
the Church, the most theologically developed is the one
that came forth from the deliberations of the Council
of Nicaea in 325 and that was slightly elaborated at the
Council of Constantinople in 381. Called the "Nicene"
or "Nicene-Constantinopolitan" Creed, it has provided
the foundation for the theological systems of most of
the great spiritual teachers of both Eastern and Western Christianity and is also used in a liturgical setting in
many of the churches, again both East and West. It is fair

to say that most Christians would subscribe to this ancient statement of our faith.

What is the meaning of this beautiful and venerable Creed? It is a statement of the fundamental pattern of the biblical form of life, and therefore the recitation or singing of it is far from an exercise in abstract theologizing. Instead, it is an existential declaration that that pattern should become the structuring pattern of one's own life.

In the opening statement, we say, *Credo in unum Deum* (I believe in one God). The unity of God is, of course, an elemental biblical claim: "Hear, O Israel: The LORD is our God, the LORD alone," says the great *shema* prayer in the sixth chapter of Deuteronomy, and monotheism, it is fair to say, is *the* distinctive mark of Jewish faith. The opening chapter of the book of Genesis, the account of the creation of all things, mentions a whole series of finite things—sun, moon, stars, animals, etc.—that in various cultures in the ancient world were worshiped as divinities. In insisting that they are creatures, the author of Genesis effectively dethrones them, placing all of them in a subordinate relation to the one God. Joseph Ratzinger has observed that the *shema* and this opening article of the Creed have in common a spiritual implication of enormous significance. To say that there is only one God or that one believes in *unum Deum* is to disempower any false claimant to ultimacy in one's life. To say that God is the only God is to say, necessarily, that no country, no political party, no human person, no movement, no ideology is of ultimate importance. It is, accordingly, to take a stand—both for and against.

We ought never to think that acceptance of the truth

of the propositions contained in the Creed is tantamount to Christian experience in its totality. On the contrary, creedal formulas are guides, guardrails, indicators on the side of the road that is leading us into God. They point us in the right direction and prevent us from going completely off the path. So, for example, if you do not believe in the Trinitarian God or in the Incarnation of the Logos or in the activity of the Holy Spirit, you are certainly in dangerous territory, and you will not tell the Christian story correctly. But the "content" of these great mysteries is not fully given in the formulas themselves; we approach that completeness only through repeated narrating of the tale and through the concrete living of the Christian life.

Part VI

Devotional Prayer

19

The Holy Hour

FULTON SHEEN deserves credit as the great prophet of the Holy Hour—a sustained, uninterrupted hour of prayer in the presence of the Blessed Sacrament. Sheen was a revered retreat director, especially for priests, and he closed every one of these spiritual exercises with the same practical recommendation: spend a Holy Hour. Many of Sheen's colleagues confirmed that, his whole life long, he remained faithful to this practice. I can personally testify that this teaching, which had been largely forgotten for a generation after his death, has been massively embraced by younger Catholics. The Holy Hour is now a staple spiritual discipline in most seminaries and in an increasing number of rectories and parishes around the country. The Holy Hour has also become a key part of my own spiritual life. When I'm home, I begin every day going to my chapel and spending an hour in prayer. That is because of Fulton J. Sheen.

What Sheen was intuiting about the importance of the Holy Hour is that it is about cultivating our relationship with Jesus. He once wrote, "Even when it seemed so unprofitable and lacking in spiritual intimacy, I still had the sensation of being at least like a dog at the master's door, ready in case he called me." He was deeply sympathetic with the description of prayer in the presence of the Blessed Sacrament once offered by a parishioner of the Curé of Ars: "I look at him and he looks at me." The Christian life is not about studying or drawing inspiration from a figure from the distant past; rather, it is about being in a personal relationship with Christ. This is realized, very powerfully, in the Holy Hour.

Once, when he was asked what one is supposed to do exactly in the presence of the Blessed Sacrament, Sheen answered: in a way, anything you want! There is no official, formalized way to spend a Holy Hour. You can pray the Liturgy of the Hours or the Rosary; you can read Scripture or spiritual works; you can prepare for teaching or preaching; you can thank God for the blessings in your life; you can bring the petitions of all those who have asked for your prayer; you can bring a pad of paper and a pencil, ready to write down the ideas and inspirations that come. You can even just sit in front of the Blessed Sacrament and do nothing at all, simply basking in his presence and undergoing a kind of "radiation therapy."

Whatever you do during the Holy Hour, the most important thing is to commit to it. Maybe you are new to the Holy Hour and need to start small or start slow. If you're a morning person like me, do this prayer right after you wake up; if you're better in the evening, do it before you go to bed. But take the time.

Stay close to Christ in the Blessed Sacrament. The Master is waiting for us; let us watch an hour with him and listen for his call.

20

The Rosary

THE LORD JESUS has entrusted his Church with privileged means through which we can participate in his victory over sin and death. These include the sacraments (especially the Eucharist and Penance), the Bible, and specific devotional prayers such as the Holy Hour and the Rosary.

The Rosary prayer actually consists of a series of smaller prayers. First, you hold the rosary and begin with the sign of the cross. Next, holding the crucifix of the rosary, you pray the ancient Apostles' Creed, which is a summary of our baptismal promises. Holding the first bead above the crucifix, you then pray the Our Father, which is the prayer that Jesus taught us to pray. For each of the three beads that follow, you pray the Hail Mary, which is derived, in part, from the greetings of the angel Gabriel and Mary's relative Elizabeth in Scripture (Luke 1:28, 42). (One thing we might pray for during this introductory triplet is an increase in faith, hope, and love.) Next, you pray the Glory Be, which gives praise to the three persons of our one God. Then you move into the heart of the Rosary: the five "decades" meditating on a certain set of mysteries in the lives of Christ and his mother: the Joyful Mysteries, the Sorrowful Mysteries, the Glorious Mysteries, and the Luminous Mysteries. After a few more prayers, you conclude in precisely the way you started: with the sign of the cross. All told, it takes about twenty or thirty minutes to pray.

Why is the Rosary so important? First, it is embodied, concrete, densely objective. It is something that you hold in your hand. The simple feel of the rosary beads can put you in a mystical frame of mind.

Second, the Rosary is a way of disciplining the mind for meditation. When our minds are skittish, superficial, obsessive, we never move to the deeper realms of the soul. The repetitious prayer of the Rosary quiets the mind and allows the depths of the soul to rise.

Third, the Rosary slows us down. For me, this is perhaps the most striking quality of the Rosary. All the spiritual traditions witness to the fact that the soul likes to go slow. The surface of the psyche is in constant motion, hurrying to its next thought. But the deep spiritual center likes to see, to hear, to savor. When we pray the Rosary, we move in a circle, arriving at the very place we started. The purpose is not to *get* particularly anywhere; rather, it is to meditate upon the great Christian mysteries, to look at the icons of Jesus' Nativity, Passion, Death, Resurrection, and Ascension from a variety of angles, in varying moods, with different emphases, the way we might muse over a Rembrandt portrait. This is just the sort of slow prayer the deep soul loves to do.

The Rosary—a concretizing, quieting, savoring prayer—has enormous spiritual power. And it therefore has enormous social and evangelical power as well. For Dorothy Day or St. Teresa of Kolkata, the link between contemplation of the divine mysteries and the most radical work on behalf of the poor was perfectly obvious. Their practical mission grew organically out of intense concentration upon sacred things. In the Rosary, we, too, join together—not only in prayer but in common purpose.

21

The Stations of the Cross

THE *VIA CRUCIS*—THE Way of the Cross or Stations of the Cross—is a wonderful way, especially during Lent, to focus the mind and heart on the literal *crux* of Christianity: the cross. Rooted in the tradition of pilgrims retracing Christ's path through Jerusalem, this intensely embodied devotion involves a retracing of fourteen scenes or "stations" of Christ's Passion and death—from being condemned to death to being laid in the tomb—through art and song, procession and gesture.

The visible stations lining the walls of almost every Catholic church in the Western world and the persistence of this devotion speak to the stubborn *cruciformity* of Christianity. In fact, if you look down at a Gothic cathedral from high above, you cannot miss one of its most remarkable characteristics: the building itself *is* a cross, the main body of the church, the "nave," constituting the upright, and the "transept" forming the great crossbeam. When pilgrims visited Notre-Dame de Paris or Chartres or Amiens, they would make their way along the walls of the church, visiting the various shrines and altars. In so doing, whether they knew it or not, they made the way of the cross, since the cross is embedded in the very structure of the place.

A confrontation with Jesus' terrible death is inescapable, inevitable. When St. Paul wanted to communicate to the Corinthians what stood at the very heart of his message, he said, "I decided to know nothing among you except Jesus Christ, and him crucified" (1 Cor. 2:2). In his first evangelical preaching recorded in the Acts of the Apostles, St. Peter sums up his proclamation: "[This man] you crucified and killed . . . God raised him up" (Acts 2:23–24). Indeed, one of the distinctive marks of Christianity vis-à-vis other great world religions is the manner of its founder's death. Mohammed died full of years, honored, and surrounded by friends and family; the Buddha died peacefully at the end of a long and eventful life, sure that his teaching would be carried on by devoted disciples. But Jesus died young, alone, abandoned even by his closest friends, by all accounts a failure, hung on a brutal instrument of torture. And this death, the first Christians insisted, was not simply a tragedy, a calamity from which we should turn our eyes, a sad end to a beautiful life; rather, somehow it was the whole point.

Even a cursory reading of the Gospels reveals that Jesus' death is the center and goal of the narrative, that which animates and gives verve to the story. It has often been remarked that the Gospels are not so much biographies of Jesus as "passion narratives with extended introductions." Jesus speaks frequently of his "hour," the culmination of his preaching and action, and this hour coincides with his coming to the cross. After his relatively peaceful Galilean ministry, Jesus "set his face to go to Jerusalem" (Luke 9:51), steeling himself for the encounter with the powers of darkness that would take place there and moving with resolution to battle. In the ironic and poetic language of the Gospel of John, the crucified Jesus is "lifted up" in the double sense of suspended above the earth and glorified. And perhaps the most disturbing mystery of the New Testament is that this culminating event of Jesus' life, this macabre glorification through crucifixion, is not simply the result of evil human choices; it is also willed by the one whom Jesus called "Abba, Father." Somehow, it is the deepest purpose of the Incarnation; somehow, it is why he was sent.

How can we make sense of this stubborn cruciformity of Christianity, set so permanently in the stone of the cathedrals? We can do so only if we remember that God *is love*. In our pride, our rebellion, our cruelty, and above all in our fear, we human beings had changed ourselves into a dysfunctional family. Designed to soar into the fullness of God, we had turned ourselves tragically inward, locking ourselves into the cramped and icy space of sin. In order to lure us out of this nightmare, God had sent the prophets and sages of Israel; through them, God had crafted covenant after covenant with us, only to see them broken, one after another. When all seemed hopeless for us, when it appeared as though the human race was doomed to self-destruction, God, who had spoken in many and varied ways, now spoke to us by his Son (see Heb. 1:1–2). God sent not simply a prophet, a representative, a plenipotentiary, but his own Self, his own heart. And this divine Son, incarnate in Jesus of Nazareth, entered the darkness and the tempest of human disorder. He went to the poor, the hungry, the self-righteous, those drunk on power and those with no power—to everyone languishing in the iciness of the far country—and he called them home.

Now, what is death but the furthest outpost of the far country and the coldest place in the Arctic landscape of sin? Therefore, the assault on death was the ultimate mission of the Son of God. There could be no place untouched by the divine mercy, no refuge from the press of God's relentless love. So God died that we might never be alone and hopeless even in this most desolate of places. When Jesus cries out "My God, my God, why have you abandoned me?" we hear not just the plea of a desperate man; we hear the agonized shout of God himself. Chesterton said it: on the cross God seemed to become an atheist. God, in Christ, knows what it is like to be left alone, in pain, sinking into the jaws of death, and therefore God becomes our friend, our brother, our fellow sufferer, even in that most terrible moment.

And this is why St. Paul can exclaim, "I am convinced that neither death, nor life, nor angels, nor rulers, nor things present, nor things to come, nor powers, nor height, nor depth, nor anything else in all creation, will be able to separate us from the love of God in Christ Jesus our Lord" (Rom. 8:38–39). Because God has established his power even at the furthest outpost of the far country, there is literally nowhere to hide from him. Because the Son has gone to the limits of godforsakenness, we run from the Father only to find ourselves, at the end of our running, in the arms of the Son. As parents would go anywhere—into prison, to a foreign land, into the gravest danger—to rescue their children, so God, the parent of the human race, went into the darkest reaches of body and soul in order to save us. And therefore, this is the meaning of the cross: God is heartbroken love.

And this is why we pray the Stations of the Cross. Jesus said that any disciple of his must be willing to take up his cross and follow the master. If God is self-forgetting love even to the point of death, then we must be such love. If God is willing to break open his own heart, then we must be willing to break open our hearts for others. The cross, in short, must become the very structure of the Christian life. We must never forget what God has done on our behalf, and we must never fail to make that love the structure and foundation of our lives.

22

The Jesus Prayer

CHRISTIAN PRAYER is an embodied business. In C.S. Lewis' *Screwtape Letters*, one of the recommendations that the training devil gives to his young charge is to encourage his "patient" to think that prayer is something very interior and mystical, having little to do with posture or the position of the body. He wants the poor man to think that whether one stands, slouches, sits, or kneels is irrelevant to the quality of one's communication with God. This, of course, is the Cartesian voice, the dualist conceit. Behind Lewis' counterposition is a very Jamesian instinct. In the *Principles of Psychology*, William James says that it is not so much sadness that makes us cry as crying that makes us feel sad, the body in a significant sense *preceding* the mind. So, when we pray, it is not so much keen feelings of devotion that force us to our knees as kneeling that gives rise to keen feelings of devotion.

The centrality of gesture, posture, and movement in the act of prayer has long been taken for granted in the Christian tradition. Thus, in the Hesychast movement in Eastern Christianity, great stress is placed upon the act of breathing while reciting the mantra-like "Jesus Prayer."

This is an adaptation of the words of the publican in Jesus' parable (Luke 18:13): "Lord Jesus Christ, Son of God, have mercy on me, a sinner." While one prays the first part of the mantra, one is encouraged to breathe in deeply, filling the lungs entirely. This act symbolizes the filling of the heart with the living presence of Christ, the placing of Jesus at the center of all that we are. At the conclusion of this first part of the prayer, one holds one's breath for a brief period and then exhales while reciting the conclusion: "Have mercy on me, a sinner." This last gesture evokes the expelling of sin from the heart. The double movement—breathing in and breathing out—is thus a sort of cleansing process, a taking in of the Holy Spirit and a letting go of unclean spirits. In certain monasteries of the Hesychast tradition, almost the whole of the monk's day is taken up with the recitation and practice of the Jesus Prayer, sometimes formally and intentionally and other times informally and instinctually.

The beauty of this prayer is that it can be practiced at any time of the day or night and in nearly any setting or circumstance. One can set aside an hour for intense and concentrated breathing prayer or one can steal two minutes in the midst of a hectic day. Or the prayer (and the feel of it in one's lungs and body) can become second nature, automatic, a constant accompaniment of one's activity and inactivity. My grandmother used to pray the Jesus Prayer in this way, breathing it out almost inaudibly whenever she sat down. However it is practiced, it is a vivid way of reminding the body of the center.

There is a spiritual classic from the Russian Orthodox tradition titled *The Way of a Pilgrim*. This little text, whose author is unknown to us, concerns a man from mid-nineteenth-century Russia who found himself deeply puzzled by St. Paul's comment in his First Letter to the Thessalonians that we should "pray without ceasing" (1 Thess. 5:17). How, he wondered, amidst all of the demands of life, is this even possible? How could the Apostle command something so patently absurd?

His botheration led him, finally, to a monastery and a conversation with an elderly spiritual teacher who revealed the secret. He taught the man the Jesus Prayer. "As you draw your breath in," he told him, "say . . . 'Lord Jesus Christ,' and as you breathe again, 'have mercy on me.'" When the searcher looked at him with some puzzlement, the elder instructed him to go back to his room and pray these words a thousand times. When the younger man returned and announced his successful completion of the task, he was told to pray it three thousand times a day, and eventually twelve thousand times. This was the manner in which the spiritual master was placing this prayer on the student's lips so that it might enter his heart and into the rhythm of his breathing in and out, and finally become so second nature to him that he was, consciously or unconsciously, praying it all the time—indeed, praying just as St. Paul had instructed the Thessalonians.

Part VII

Scriptural Prayer

23

Lectio Divina

A PARTICULARLY EFFECTIVE MEANS of immersing oneself prayerfully in the biblical texts is the ancient practice of *lectio divina* (sacred reading), a discipline that Pope Benedict XVI warmly recommends in *Verbum Domini*. Like the Liturgy of the Hours, it has its roots in an ancient monastic practice, as a large part of the monk's day would be taken up with this task of prayerfully reading the Word of God. But because it's very simple and very clear, it's a great option for someone who is just starting to pray in a more disciplined way.

Lectio divina consists, classically, of four steps: *lectio*, *meditatio*, *oratio*, and *contemplatio*. First is *lectio* (reading)—a slow and careful reading of a text of Scripture. Let's say you're just starting out with prayer. Is there a Scripture passage you've heard that you particularly love? Is there a biblical story you've read about that you particularly relate to? Now take a brief section of that passage and read it—not in the way you read the newspaper or an article, skimming it just to get the basic idea; no, read it slowly, carefully, and with deep spiritual attention, looking at the words and mulling them over. You might even read it multiple times, concentrating on its rhythms, its odd words, its distinctive turns of phrase, perhaps taking it with each breath one phrase at a time.

Next comes *meditatio* (meditation)—a searching out of the meaning of a text. After you have read with exquisite care, isolate one word or one phrase—or maybe two or three, but no more—that especially struck you or puzzled you or made you think twice. Then ruminate on it—from the Latin *ruminare*, meaning "to chew the cud" (a favorite image of the medieval masters). Like an animal getting all the juices out of its cud, stay with it for a while: weigh it, consider it, turn it over, throw it up in the air, let it catch the light in different ways. What are the overtones and undertones? What associations can you make? What is the symbolic depth of that word or phrase? What does it remind you of in other parts of the Bible?

Having read and ruminated on the Scripture, you are now ready for *oratio* (prayer), speaking to the Lord in response to his Word. All prayer is a dialogue between ourselves and God. In the Word, we are addressed by God and spoken to personally by him; now, we speak back to him. Tell him what is on your mind and heart: How has this Scripture passage challenged, excited, or inspired you? What questions do you have about it? Ask, "Lord, why have you given me this word? Why have you invited me to ruminate on this phrase? What are you saying precisely to me?" The word is an address in love, and your *oratio* is a response in love.

The final step could be seen as the culmination of step three: *contemplatio* (contemplation), hearing what the Lord has said in response to prayer. Having read, meditated, and spoken, now it's time to listen to what

God is going to say to you. This is not so much an active step like *meditatio* or even *oratio*; it is a much more passive, receptive one. In contemplation, we simply rest in the presence of God—beyond speech, beyond imagery, beyond words, but in the space somehow opened up by the words of the Bible. I love and am loved, and that is enough.

So, in summary: first, read the scriptural text carefully; second, pick out one word or one passage that specially struck you, meditating on it; third, speak to God, telling him how your heart was moved by what you read; fourth and finally, listen to the Lord, discerning what he speaks back to you. Through this dialogic reading of the Scripture, one appropriates the Bible in the presence and under the guidance of that book's principal author—namely, God.

This process could take you twenty minutes, a half hour, or even an hour. But if you spend time with these four steps of *lectio divina*, culminating in this great act of contemplative listening to what God wants to tell you, the Bible will spring to life.

24

The Our Father

THE LORD'S PRAYER or "Our Father," found in the Gospel of Matthew and, in shorter form, the Gospel of Luke (Matt. 6:9–13; Luke 11:2–4), is the most beloved and popular prayer in the Christian tradition. It is a prayer for the Christian journey, one that has been offered up consistently for the past two thousand years and continues to be offered millions of times every day around the world. Think for a moment how this prayer links us to all of the great figures in Christian history, from Peter and Paul to Augustine, Thomas Aquinas, Francis of Assisi, John Henry Newman, G.K. Chesterton, John Paul II, right up to the present day.

These words of Jesus are of great moment, for in them, the Son of God—not just a guru, spiritual teacher, or religious genius, but the very Word made flesh—teaches us to pray. This is why the Our Father is the model of all prayer. How wonderful, too, that it comes directly from the prayer of Jesus himself. In Luke, we hear that he has been spending significant time in prayer before the disciples ask him how to pray. It is as though the prayer that he teaches them sums up the content of his own prayer. So let us attend carefully to his words.

First, "Our Father, who art in heaven, hallowed be thy name." From the time of the fall, our basic problem is getting our priorities mixed up. We desire and seek all kinds of worldly things—money, pleasure, power, honor—that are ephemeral and unsatisfying. What we should desire, first, is God. This is precisely what the prayer to make holy (hallowed) the name of God is all about. It's not that God's name isn't in fact holy; we're praying that we might keep it that way, that we might honor God in and above all things, that he might be the highest value in our lives. We're praying for a radical reorientation of our consciousness. In a sense, everything else in the spiritual life flows from this prioritization: "Hear, O Israel: The LORD is our God, the LORD alone" (Deut. 6:4); "Love the LORD your God with all your heart, and with all your soul, and with all your mind" (Matt. 22:37). If we get this wrong, we get everything else wrong.

And who precisely is this God whom we are making central? Not Tyrant, King, or Emperor, but Father—the one who creates and sustains us, who governs us and provides for us, who directs us finally back to him. The same intimacy that Jesus has with his *Abba* ("Daddy"), he invites us to share. We don't just imitate his prayer the way we would imitate the prayer of any spiritual teacher; rather, we enter into the dynamics of his own being. But notice the wonderful tension that is established from the beginning: God is addressed with great intimacy as our *Abba*, but we remind ourselves that he exists "in heaven." This, of course, is a metaphorical way of speaking. Don't think of God as literally inhabiting a corner of the sky or of distant space. Since God creates the world, he is not anything or anybody in the world. He is not one being among many, but rather the transcendent source of all that is. What we see on display here is the play between God's immanence and transcendence, which is key in the spiritual order.

Then we ask, "Thy kingdom come, thy will be done on earth as it is in heaven." The kingdom stood at the very center of Jesus' life and teaching. It is the reign of God for which Israel had longed for a thousand years. In the face of the trials, injustices, pain, and suffering of this world, Israel began to dream that one day God would reign and would set things right. God would be the righteous king of the world.

The kingdom thus means something like "God's order" or "God's way of doing things." It means the created realm mirroring the mind and purpose of God. Jesus is, as Origen said, *autobasileia*, the kingdom in person. His teaching and indeed his whole manner of life gives us a very good idea of what this kingdom would look like: peace, nonviolence, inclusion of the outsider, forgiveness, healing, walking the path of compassion. That's the kingdom, the order that mimics the order that obtains within the community of the Trinity. We pray, therefore, that we, as members of his Mystical Body, might have our wills aligned to this great purpose, that we might be steeled to this mission, that we might not give in to the "world," the ways of the earthly kingdom. We pray that the ways of love, mercy, compassion, justice, forgiveness, and nonviolence obtain here below as they already do in heaven. In short, we are praying that Jesus' manner of being becomes, more and more, the manner of being of the world.

This petition links us to the heavenly world of the angels and saints, the rightly ordered community. Do we make this desire central to our work, our family life, our business dealings, our recreation? Do we really desire that God's order obtains here and now? Pray this prayer as you go off to work. Pray it as you commence your day. Pray it as you face a difficult decision. Pray it when you are tempted.

Then comes a mysterious petition: "Give us this day our daily bread." This seems to be the most straightforward request in the prayer, but it is actually quite puzzling. The Greek phrase that stands behind this is *ton arton ton epiousion*. *Arton* refers to bread, but what does *epiousion* mean? This highly ambiguous and rare Greek word exists nowhere else in Greek literature and is found only in the two Gospel passages with the Lord's Prayer; hence, even some of the early Fathers, whose native language was Greek, were not entirely sure. It is rendered as "daily," but the literal sense is "super-substantial."

What is this extraordinary bread that Jesus asks us to pray for? Some have speculated that it means the bread that we need for the day, just enough to get us through from day to day. Others say that the "day" in question refers to the eschatological day, the final day of salvation. But I think the best way to think about it is along Eucharistic lines. What is the Eucharist? Not ordinary bread, not simply a symbolic representation, but rather the transubstantiated presence of the Body and Blood of Jesus. The Church speaks of a change not at the level of appearance but at the level of substance. What we are asking for, therefore, is the Eucharist, this intimate communion with the living Christ. This is the bread of eternal life.

Especially in the modern period, we have become un-comfortable with the organic side of Christianity—that mystical dimension of our faith that invites us to partic-ipate in the lifeblood of God. We're at home with a sense of religion as moral rectitude and spiritual alertness, but this prayer is telling us that there is more to it than that. We should pray for the Eucharistic bread that readies us for eternal life, that food which renders us participants in God's own nature; food at a higher pitch of perfection; food that feeds the soul as much as the body; food that is the very Body and Blood of Jesus.

Next, we ask God to remove those obstacles that keep us from union with him: "And forgive us our tres-passes." Sin blocks union with God; it keeps the king-dom from coming; it is inimical to the bread of life. That is why we beg God to eliminate it from our lives. Jesus came for many reasons and accomplished many things. He taught us the way of love; he embodied what it means to live as a servant of the Lord; he healed; he performed miracles. But what he came to do, first and foremost, was to forgive our sins: "Son, your sins are forgiven" (Mark 2:5); "Neither do I condemn you" (John 8:11). And on the cross, what took place was the definitive act of sacrifice by which humanity is reconciled to divinity. The Lamb of God took away the sins of the world. And so, we are praying for the forgiveness of Christ. We have to beg for forgiveness.

And then right away we draw the proper implica-tion: "as we forgive those who trespass against us." One of the faces of sin is precisely our unwillingness to for-give others. How central to the teaching of Jesus is for-giveness! And how central to the suffering of the world is our incapacity to forgive. Think of all the suffering in the world, from the smallest, most intimate level to the grandest geopolitical scale; what we find, over and over again, is the incapacity to forgive, the persistence of poisoned memory. Forgiveness is not simply a velleity; it is the active repairing of broken relationships.

How wonderful and how deeply challenging that at the very heart of the prayer that the Son of God taught us is a petition to be given the grace to forgive. What is our task but to embody the work of Jesus—to become, ourselves, agents of forgiveness? We are asking that there be a coordination between the lavish way that God has forgiven us and the manner in which we forgive others who have harmed us. And so, as you pray this section of the prayer, call to mind your sins and how generous God has been to you, and think of the broken relationships that you could do something to heal.

Finally, we pray, "And lead us not into temptation, but deliver us from evil." The last petition of the Lord's Prayer acknowledges that we are in a spiritual warfare. There was a kind of giddy optimism that seized the Church after Vatican II, and it wasn't good for us. There are myriad forces in the world that are opposed to God's kingdom, and they do not rest. More to it, there is a dimension to evil that is not readily apparent to us. As Paul pointed out, our real battle is "not against enemies of blood and flesh, but against the rulers, against the authorities, against the cosmic powers of this present darkness, against the spiritual forces of evil in the heavenly places" (Eph. 6:12). We mustn't be naïve about these forces, physical and spiritual, that are opposed to us and that seek to draw us to themselves. We must instead invoke the mighty power of God to prevent us from being tempted and to liberate us from *ho poneros*, the Evil One.

Can you see, in conclusion, how the entire prayer is a prayer for Christ? We pray that his kingdom might come; that we might commune with his Body and Blood; that we might receive his forgiveness; that we might accept him wholeheartedly. And can you see how this prayer rightly orders us? We must put God's holy name first; we must strive to do his will in all things and at all times; we must be strengthened by spiritual food or we will fall; we must be agents of forgiveness; we must be able to withstand the dark powers.

25

The Psalms

I ONCE HAD THE EXTRAORDINARY EXPERIENCE of recording all 150 Psalms for Hallow, a Catholic prayer app. Over the course of several sittings, sequestered in a tiny studio, I endeavored to communicate the intelligence, passion, and devotion of the person (more likely persons) who wrote these ancient poems. Though I have been regularly praying the Psalms as part of the Liturgy of the Hours for the past roughly forty years, I had never before simply read them through aloud, one after another. It was, at the same time, demanding and deeply prayerful—and it compelled me to see the Psalms with fresh eyes.

As I pronounced these poems from the Church's privileged book of prayer, I thought frequently of Dietrich von Hildebrand's musings on the heart. Von Hildebrand complained that the Catholic intellectual tradition gives ample attention to the mind and to the will but that it painfully neglects the heart—which is to say, the seat of the passions and emotions. In the presence of a value, he says, the entire person responds, the mind appreciating what is true in it, the will seeking what is good in it, and the heart delighting in its beauty. This multivalent "value response" occurs in relation to, say, Beethoven's Seventh Symphony, a pristine winter morning, a lovely face, or an elegant mathematical equation. And it occurs, *par excellence*, with respect to the supreme value of God. The mind revels in God's truth (think of the writings of Thomas Aquinas); the will responds to God's infinite goodness (think of the dedication of Maximilian Kolbe or the Little Flower); and the heart overflows in the presence of his splendor (think of the words and gestures of the liturgy).

Now, there is indeed something of Aquinas in the Psalms, for we could distill a theology of God from them; and there is indeed something of Kolbe in them, for we could tease from them a moral program; but there is in them, above all, the aching, longing, and delight of the heart. The Psalmist exults, laments, spits out his anger, excoriates his enemies, praises God and berates God; he is so happy he can barely contain himself, and he is so profoundly sad that he feels like lying down with dead people. The motto that St. John Henry Newman took when he became a cardinal was *Cor ad cor loquitur* (Heart speaks to heart). I can't think of a better description of what is happening as we recite the Psalms: to the God who has poured out his heart to us, we pour out our own hearts.

A second strong impression I had upon reading all the Psalms is how much stress they place on enemies. I would wager that "enemy" and "foe" are among the most common words in the book of Psalms. Again and again, the author agonizes over those who are opposed to him; those who threaten him, both with speech and with swords; those who plot against him; those who make him the object of their mockery; those who would be glad to see him in his grave; etc. Moreover, the Psalmist actively wants their destruction, their defeat, their humiliation; he even wants to bash in the heads of their children! The reader of the Psalms might be forgiven for thinking that the author of these texts is more than a touch paranoid.

But I don't think that psychologizing the Psalmist is nearly as interesting as musing on the theology that provides the context for his preoccupation with his foes. The simple truth is that, in a fallen world, the righteous man will have enemies, and the more righteous he is, the more of them he will have. The person with no enemies is not to be trusted, for he stands for nothing. There is, of course, no better example of this principle than Jesus himself in relation to his contemporaries. As the Gospels unfold, we see the army of Jesus' antagonists increasing exponentially, and by the end of the narrative, those opponents put him to death. So intense is the opposition to him that we can speak of the sins of the world being placed upon him. To be sure, Jesus consistently urged the love of one's enemies, and, from the cross, he uttered a word of forgiveness to those who were putting him to death. But as Stanley Hauerwas quipped, in order to love one's enemies, one has to have some enemies. It is difficult to read the Psalms and not come to grips with these peculiar dynamics.

A third and final point I would like to make is that the Psalms give expression to the distinctively dialogic quality of biblical religion. It is a commonplace to say that Christianity is a revealed religion—which is to say, one based not so much on philosophical speculation or mythological imagination but on the speech of God to us.

A divine person has addressed us, and therefore it is only natural that we should speak back—in praise, thanksgiving, frustration, puzzlement, and grief. The Psalms, perhaps more than any other book in the Bible, display this conversational quality of biblical faith. And, therefore, it is perfectly appropriate that the Church has used the Psalms liturgically as the optimal way to respond to the Word of God. Though they are often obscured by bad lectors or set to tragically treacly melodies, the Responsorial Psalms at Mass are just that: the privileged manner in which we speak back to the God who has spoken to us. It was actually a peculiarly thrilling thing that, as I read aloud these ancient texts and felt the emotion of the author, I sensed that I was indeed conversing with the mysterious one who had first broached the conversation.

So, if you feel that your spiritual life has grown a bit dry, or if you sense that you have wandered away from the God who loves you, I might recommend that you open up the Church's songbook—and sing.

26

The De Profundis

ANCIENT PEOPLES hated traveling by sea. They were, for very good reason, frightened of the depths, especially given the terrible state of transport in those days. Even experienced sailors hugged the shore whenever they could. Therefore, it's not surprising that, when biblical people wanted to conjure up their deepest anxieties, their most terrible spiritual and psychological states, they would speak of the roaring and untamed sea.

So, for example, in the book of Genesis, we hear of the *tohu wabohu* or "formless void" (Gen. 1:2)—the primal, unformed chaos out of which God draws creation. We hear, in the book of Exodus, of the frightening Red Sea, which blocks the Israelite escape from Egypt. And in all four of the Gospels, there is a version of the story of the storm at sea. Karl Barth said that the stormy waters in all of these cases stand for *das Nichtige*, the nothing, that which stands opposed to God's creative intentions, difficulties both interior and exterior, both physical and psychological—all the darkness that surrounds us in life.

In the story of the storm at sea, the disciples in the boat are evocative of the Church, making its way through time and space. And those waters are symbolic of everything that besets the members of the Church. To stay within the emotional space of the story, this must have been a terrible storm to have terrified experienced sailors. Therefore, it does not stand for a minor problem, but rather a major, overwhelming, life-threatening struggle. And in the midst of that storm, they cry out: "Lord, save us!" "Master, Master, we are perishing!" "Do you not care that we are perishing?" (Matt. 8:25; Luke 8:24; Mark 4:38).

The *de profundis* prayer, Latin for "out of the depths," comes from Psalm 130: "Out of the depths I cry to you, O Lord. Lord, hear my voice! Let your ears be attentive to the voice of my supplications!" It is the prayer offered at the darkest times of life, when we find ourselves lost and in the shadow of death, when, in our desperation, we feel utterly incapable of helping or saving ourselves. "Out of the depths I cry to you, O Lord."

In their wonderful book on the history of prayer, Philip and Carol Zaleski speak a great deal about this kind of prayer. A good example is John Newton, the author of the hymn "Amazing Grace," who offered a *de profundis* prayer when he found himself in the middle of the Atlantic Ocean, the ship caught in a violent storm. Knowing that he was spiritually lost and in a morally hopeless situation, in the midst of that great ocean, he prayed a *de profundis* prayer, and his life was changed; he experienced amazing grace. The Zaleskis talk about Daniel Defoe's novel *Robinson Crusoe*, which is much more than an adventure story; it is ultimately, they argue, a spiritual adventure story—a strict allegory of the Christian life. Crusoe is stranded on a desert island and thinks he's lost everything. He's able to salvage from the sinking ship a few basic things, one of which is a Bible. For the longest time during his trial, he ignores the Bible, but then, in the midst of his despair, this unreligious man, unaccustomed to prayer, prays a version of the *de profundis* prayer, and through that prayer, his life changes; his attitudes, perspective, and fortunes change.

One of the most moving stories that they recount is that of Bill Wilson, the founder of Alcoholics Anonymous. Bill was a bright and gifted man who found himself to be completely the prisoner of alcohol. He would lose job after job; try every kind of treatment, both physical and psychological; and get back on his feet, only to fall again. The terrible pattern of addiction repeated itself so often that he found himself in utter despair, contemplating suicide. It was then, when he was at rock bottom, that he encountered a friend who spoke in glowing terms of a religious way out of addiction, one mediated by prayer. In the detox center, at the end of his rope, having tried everything, despairing of a solution, he prayed the *de profundis* prayer, and he experienced a spiritual awakening, and from that moment on, he never drank again. The twelve-step program—admitting your powerlessness before the addiction, but then turning your life over to a higher power—was born from this profoundly spiritual experience. At rock bottom, you're able to pray, quite literally, from the depths.

What we hear in the story of the calming of the storm at sea is the great New Testament version of the *de profundis* prayer, offered by the Church in its desperation: *O Lord, we're drowning! Don't you care? Lord, wake up! Don't you see the situation we're in? God, help us!* Perhaps there are some people reading this right now who find themselves in these depths. Maybe you are reading these words in prison; indeed, one of the most powerful *de profundis* prayers is one that the writer Oscar Wilde composed in prison after falling from the pinnacle of British society. Maybe you're reading these words from your hospital bed, where you are recovering painfully from surgery or where you've just received some devastating news about your health. Maybe you find yourself caught in a terrible, unrelenting depression; maybe you've tried all sorts of cures, physical and psychological, and nothing seems to work. Maybe you've just lost a loved one, and you find yourself awash in a sea of grief.

We're not talking about having a difficult day; we're talking about being in the depths. Please identify yourself right now with the disciples in the boat, and do what they did: knowing your helplessness, cry out, and pray the *de profundis* prayer. For what happened to the disciples? Jesus awakens, and he calms the storm. There hovers over the *tohu wabohu*, Genesis tells us, the Spirit of God, and in Jesus, we see that God made flesh. Christ is the very incarnate power of God who—though he is in the same boat with us—can hover sovereignly over even the greatest difficulties of life. Cry out to him! Offer this prayer from the heart and from the depths, and awaken Christ to calm the storm.

Notes

Part I: What Is Prayer?

1: Raising the Mind and Heart to God

Source: Robert Barron, *Catholicism: A Journey to the Heart of the Faith* (New York: Image Books, 2011), 224–225.

3 **"Prayer is the raising of one's mind and heart to God"**: Quoted in *Catechism of the Catholic Church* 2590, vatican.va.

3 **"a surge of the heart"**: Quoted in *Catechism of the Catholic Church* 2558.

4 **as Herbert McCabe argued so clearly**: See Herbert McCabe, *God Matters* (London: Continuum, 2005), 220.

4 **God's self-communication, given in grace, and accepted in freedom**: See Karl Rahner, *Grace in Freedom* (New York: Herder and Herder, 1969), 231.

4 **a contemporary commentator on St. John of the Cross**: Iain Matthew, *The Impact of God: Soundings from St. John of the Cross* (London: Hodder and Stoughton, 1995), 35.

5 **"Prayer is such an easy job!"**: Paul Murray, *Preachers at Prayer: Soundings in the Dominican Spiritual Tradition* (Elk Grove Village, IL: Word on Fire, 2024), 6.

2: A Conversation Between Friends

Source: Bishop Robert Barron, "Bishop Barron on Prayer,"

YouTube video, February 16, 2017, https://www.youtube.com /watch?v=aR6J1pPiRQo.

6 "Take the time": See *The Pocket Thomas Merton*, ed. Robert Inchausti (Boulder, CO: Shambala, 2017), 54.

9 "the fruit of service is peace": Mother Teresa, *Where There Is Love, There Is God*, ed. Brian Kolodiejchuk (New York: Image, 2010), 16.

3: The Christian Difference

Source: "169: The Metaphysics of Prayer," *Word on Fire Show* podcast, March 4, 2019, https://www.wordonfire.org/videos /wordonfire-show/episode169/; Robert Barron, *The Strangest Way: Walking the Christian Path* (Park Ridge, IL: Word on Fire Institute, 2021), 58–59.

13 Charles Williams took as the elemental principle: Charles Williams, *Essential Writings in Spirituality and Theology*, ed. Charles Hefling (Cambridge, MA: Cowley, 1993), 204–230.

4: The Disorienting Quality of Prayer

Source: Robert Barron, "The Disorienting Quality of Real Prayer," Word on Fire, March 15, 2016, https://www.wordonfire .org/articles/barron/the-disorienting-quality-of-real-prayer/.

14 A first such exercise, Murdoch suggests, is the learning of a foreign language: Iris Murdoch, *The Sovereignty of Good* (New York: Schocken Books, 1971), 89.

15 A second spiritual exercise recommended by Iris Murdoch: Iris Murdoch, *The Sovereignty of Good* (New York: Schocken Books, 1971), 85–88.

16 James Joyce brilliantly displays the dynamics of confronting the truly beautiful: James Joyce, *A Portrait of the Artist as a Young Man* (New York: B.W. Huebsch, 1916), 199–200.

5: Transfigured Prayer

Source: Unpublished homily text.

22 "cloud of unknowing": *The Cloud of Unknowing*, ed. James Walsh, Classics of Western Spirituality (Mahwah, NJ: Paulist, 1981).

Part II: Principles of Prayer

6: The Four Rules of Prayer

Source: Robert Barron, *Proclaiming the Power of Christ: Classic Sermons* (Park Ridge, IL: Word on Fire Institute, 2021), 116–120.

7: Why We Should Address Jesus as Thou

Source: Robert Barron, "Why We Should Address Jesus as Thou," Word on Fire, November 22, 2016, https://www.wordonfire.org/articles/barron/why-we-should-address-jesus-as-thou/.

30 Archbishop Sartain relayed a story reported by Catherine's spiritual director, Raymond of Capua: Raymond of Capua, *The Life of Saint Catherine of Siena*, trans. George Lamb (New York: P.J. Kenedy and Sons, 1960), 96.

30 "Glory be to the Father, and to Thee, and to the Holy Ghost!": Johannes Jørgensen, *Saint Catherine of Siena*, trans. Ingeborg Lund (Eugene, OR: Wipf & Stock, 2012), 56–57.

8: The Prayers of the Saints

Source: Robert Barron, "Satellites, the Internet, and the Communion of Saints," Word on Fire, October 4, 2016, https://www.wordonfire.org/articles/barron/satellites-the-internet-and-the-communion-of-saints/.

36 the soul is in the body "not as contained by it, but as containing it": Thomas Aquinas, *Summa theologiae* 1.52.1.

37 "You, eternal shepherd, do not desert your flock, but through the blessed Apostles, watch over it and protect it": *Roman Missal* (ICEL, 2010).

Part III: Types of Prayer

9: Contrition and Cleansing of the Temple

Source: Unpublished homily text.

10: Adoration and Right Praise

Source: Robert Barron, *2 Samuel* (Grand Rapids, MI: Brazos, 2015), 50–52.

46 not only as a cry of erotic desire but also as a longing of the soul for worship: Bernard of Clairvaux, "Sermons on the Song of Songs," in *Bernard of Clairvaux: Selected Works*, trans. G.R. Evans (New York: Paulist, 1987), 213.

46 "Cult cultivates the culture": Dorothy Day, *The Long Loneliness: The Autobiography of Dorothy Day* (Chicago: Thomas More, 1952), 203.

47 right praise ... is tantamount to human flourishing:

Matthew Levering, *Ezra and Nehemiah* (Grand Rapids, MI: Brazos, 2007), 19.

48 he consistently coupled covenant with sacrificial worship: Matthew Levering, *Ezra and Nehemiah* (Grand Rapids, MI: Brazos, 2007), 51–52.

48 The action of bringing an animal to the tabernacle: Margaret Barker, *The Great High Priest: The Temple Roots of Christian Liturgy* (London: T&T Clark, 2003), 53.

11: Give Thanks in All Circumstances

Source: Unpublished homily text.

51 the sheer act of being itself: Thomas Aquinas, *Summa theologiae* 1.3.4.

51 as Jean-Pierre de Caussade put it, everything that happens to us: Jean-Pierre de Caussade, *Abandonment to Divine Providence: With Letters of Father de Caussade on the Practice of Self-Abandonment*, trans. E.J. Strickland (San Francisco: Ignatius, 2011).

12: Prayer of Petition

Source: Robert Barron, *Catholicism: A Journey to the Heart of the Faith* (New York: Image Books, 2011), 243–246.

55 St. Augustine offers another perspective on our dilemma: Augustine, *Letters* 130.8–9 (NPNF1 1:463–465).

56 "accepted the motherly tears of Saint Monica": *Roman Missal* (ICEL, 2010).

Part IV: Contemplative Prayer

13: John of the Cross and the Dark Night of the Soul

Source: Robert Barron, *Catholicism: A Journey to the Heart of the Faith* (New York: Image Books, 2011), 232–238.

64 Consider these gorgeous lines from John's poem on the dark night: John of the Cross, *Ascent of Mount Carmel*, in *The Collected Works of St. John of the Cross*, trans. Kieran Kavanaugh and Otilio Rodriguez (Washington, DC: ICS Publications, 2017), 113–114.

14: Teresa of Avila and Finding the Center

Source: Robert Barron, *Catholicism: A Journey to the Heart of the Faith* (New York: Image Books, 2011), 239–242.

67 the "transverberation," which Teresa vividly describes in her autobiography: Teresa of Avila, *The Book of Her Life*, trans. Kieran Kavanaugh and Otilio Rodriguez (Indianapolis, IN: Hackett, 2008), 200.

68 shout "to the hard of hearing": Flannery O'Connor, "The Fiction Writer & His Country," in *Flannery O'Connor Collection*, ed. Matthew Becklo (Park Ridge, IL: Word on Fire Classics, 2019), 412.

69 the *Seelengrund* (the ground of the soul): Meister Eckhart, "Sermon 21," in *Meister Eckhart: Teacher and Preacher*, ed. Bernard McGinn (Mahwah, NJ: Paulist, 1986), 281.

69 "inner wine cellar": John of the Cross, *The Spiritual Canticle*, in *The Collected Works of St. John of the Cross*, trans. Kieran Kavanaugh and Otilio Rodriguez (Washington, DC: ICS Publications, 2017), 574–580.

70 **"We must make ourselves indifferent to all created things":** Ignatius of Loyola, *The Spiritual Exercises*, in *Ignatian Collection*, ed. Daniel Seseske (Park Ridge, IL: Word on Fire Classics, 2020), 22–23.

70 **"Let nothing disturb you":** "Bookmark of St. Teresa of Avila," Catholic Culture, https://www.catholicculture.org /culture/liturgicalyear/prayers/view.cfm?id=874.

15: Thomas Merton and the Virginal Point

Source: Robert Barron, *Catholicism: A Journey to the Heart of the Faith* (New York: Image Books, 2011), 225–226, 246–249.

72 **Merton spoke of *le point vierge* (the virginal point):** Thomas Merton, *Conjectures of a Guilty Bystander* (New York: Image, 2009), 155–156.

72 **finding that place in you where you are here and now being created:** See Thomas Merton, *New Seeds of Contemplation* (New York: New Directions, 1961), 1–5.

72 **Étienne Gilson's notion of the divine aseity:** Étienne Gilson, *The Spirit of Medieval Philosophy*, trans. A.H.C. Downes (New York: Charles Scribner's Sons, 1940), 53–54.

74 **"they are all walking around shining like the sun":** Thomas Merton, *Conjectures of a Guilty Bystander* (New York: Image, 2009), 153–155.

Part V: Liturgical Prayer

16: The Mass

Source: Robert Barron, *The Strangest Way: Walking the Christian Path* (Park Ridge, IL: Word on Fire Institute, 2021), 178–182.

77 **"the source and summit of the Christian life":** Vatican Council II, *Sacrosanctum Concilium* 10, in *The Word on Fire Vatican II Collection: Constitutions*, ed. Matthew Levering (Park Ridge, IL: Word on Fire Institute, 2021), 160.

77 **"It is a kind of ballet, with similar prescribed movements and gestures":** Edward Rice, *The Man in the Sycamore Tree: The Good Times and Hard Life of Thomas Merton* (New York: Image Books, 1972), 97.

78 **what the council fathers at Vatican II called the "heavenly liturgy":** *Sacrosanctum Concilium* 8, in *The Word on Fire Vatican II Collection: Constitutions*, ed. Matthew Levering (Park Ridge, IL: Word on Fire Institute, 2021), 158.

81 **in the great "Holy, holy, holy":** This and the following quotations from the Mass from *Roman Missal* (ICEL, 2010).

17: The Liturgy of the Hours

Source: "332: How to Start Praying the Liturgy of the Hours," *Word on Fire Show* podcast, April 18, 2022, https://www.wordonfire.org/videos/wordonfire-show/episode332/.

84 **The mission of the laity is . . . to go out and sanctify the world:** Vatican Council II, *Lumen Gentium* 30–38, in *The Word on Fire Vatican II Collection: Constitutions*, ed. Matthew Levering (Park Ridge, IL: Word on Fire Institute, 2021), 89–100; Vatican Council II, *Apostolicam Actuositatem*, in *The Word on Fire Vatican II Collection: Decrees and Declarations*, ed. Matthew Levering (Elk Grove Village, IL: Word on Fire Institute, 2023), 273–325.

86 **the complexity of navigating the texts:** For a helpful alternative, try Word on Fire's Liturgy of the Hours monthly subscription booklet: https://www.wordonfire.org/pray/.

18: The Creed

Source: Robert Barron, *Light from Light: A Theological Reflection on the Nicene Creed* (Park Ridge, IL: Word on Fire Academic, 2021), 21–22, 7; Robert Barron, *Bridging the Great Divide: Musings of a Post-Liberal, Post-Conservative Evangelical Catholic* (Lanham, MD: Rowman & Littlefield, 2004), 44–45.

88 Joseph Ratzinger has observed that the *shema*: Joseph Ratzinger, *Introduction to Christianity*, 2nd ed. (San Francisco: Ignatius, 2004), 110–115.

Part VI: Devotional Prayer

19: The Holy Hour

Source: Robert Barron, foreword to *The Holy Hour: Meditations for Eucharistic Adoration*, ed. Matthew Becklo (Park Ridge, IL: Word on Fire, 2022), ix–xi.

94 "like a dog at the master's door": Fulton Sheen, *Treasure in Clay: The Autobiography of Fulton J. Sheen* (New York: Image Books, 2008), 202.

94 "I look at him and he looks at me": See *Catechism of the Catholic Church* 2715.

20: The Rosary

Source: Bishop Robert Barron, "Why Pray the Rosary?" YouTube video, February 25, 2021, https://www.youtube.com /watch?v=vE247jOt4AA.

21: The Stations of the Cross

Source: Robert Barron, *Heaven in Stone and Glass: Experiencing the Spirituality of the Great Cathedrals* (New York: Crossroad, 2002), 37–41, 43.

99 **"passion narratives with extended introductions"**: This phrase was first used by the German theologian Martin Kähler in 1892 in *Der sogenannte historische Jesus und der geschichtliche, biblische Christus*. The work appears in English as *The So-Called Historical Jesus and the Historic, Biblical Christ*, ed. Carl Braaten (Philadelphia: Fortress, 1964), 80, n. 11.

101 **Chesterton said it: on the cross God seemed to become an atheist:** G.K. Chesterton, *Orthodoxy* (Park Ridge, IL: Word on Fire Classics, 2017), 140.

22: The Jesus Prayer

Source: Robert Barron, *The Strangest Way: Walking the Christian Path* (Park Ridge, IL: Word on Fire Institute, 2021), 55–57; Robert Barron, "A Pilgrim, a Bishop, and His iPhone," Word on Fire, November 15, 2016, https://www.wordonfire.org/articles/barron/a-pilgrim-a-bishop-and-his-iphone/.

103 **In C.S. Lewis'** *Screwtape Letters***:** C.S. Lewis, *The Screwtape Letters* (London: Geoffrey Bles, 1945), 24–25.

103 **William James says that it is not so much sadness that makes us cry:** William James, *The Principles of Psychology*, vol. 2 (New York: Henry Holt, 1923), 449–450.

105 **"say . . . 'Lord Jesus Christ,' and as you breathe again, 'have mercy on me'":** *The Way of a Pilgrim*, trans. R.M. French (London: SPCK, 1982), 102.

Part VII: Scriptural Prayer

23: *Lectio Divina*

Source: "031: 5 Ways to Prayer Better Today," *Word on Fire Show* podcast, July 12, 2016, https://www.wordonfire.org/videos /wordonfire-show/episode31/.

109   a discipline that Pope Benedict XVI warmly recommends in *Verbum Domini*: Benedict XVI, *Verbum Domini* 86–87, post-synodal apostolic exhortation, September 30, 2010, vatican.va.

24: The Our Father

Source: Unpublished homily text.

114 Jesus is, as Origen said, *autobasileia*, the kingdom in person: Origen, *Commentary on Matthew* 14.7.

25: The Psalms

Source: Robert Barron, "The Church's Song Book," Word on Fire, February 1, 2022, https://www.wordonfire.org/articles /barron/the-psalms-the-churchs-song-book/.

119 Dietrich von Hildebrand's musings on the heart: Dietrich von Hildebrand, *The Heart: An Analysis of Human and Divine Affectivity* (South Bend, IN: St. Augustine's Press, 2007).

26: The *De Profundis*

Source: Unpublished homily text.

123 Karl Barth said that the stormy waters in all of these cases stand for *das Nichtige*: Karl Barth, "God and Nothingness," in

Church Dogmatics, vol. 3.3, *The Doctrine of Creation, Sections 50–51*, ed. G.W. Bromiley and T.F. Torrance (London: T&T Clark, 2010), 1–78.

124 A good example is John Newton, the author of the hymn "Amazing Grace": Philip Zaleski and Carol Zaleski, *Prayer: A History* (Boston: Houghton Mifflin, 2005), 109.

124 The Zaleskis talk about Daniel Defoe's novel *Robinson Crusoe*: Philip Zaleski and Carol Zaleski, *Prayer: A History* (Boston: Houghton Mifflin, 2005), 102–109.

125 Bill Wilson, the founder of Alcoholics Anonymous: Philip Zaleski and Carol Zaleski, *Prayer: A History* (Boston: Houghton Mifflin, 2005), 120–127.

126 that the writer Oscar Wilde composed in prison: Philip Zaleski and Carol Zaleski, *Prayer: A History* (Boston: Houghton Mifflin, 2005), 119.